Successful
BRANDING

Successful
BRANDING

Pran K Choudhury

Universities Press

Universities Press (India) Limited

Registered Office
3-5-819 Hyderguda, Hyderabad 500 029 (A.P.), India

Distributed by
Orient Longman Limited

Registered Office
3-6-272 Himayatnagar, Hyderabad 500 029 (A.P.), India

Other Offices
Bangalore / Bhopal / Bhubaneshwar / Calcutta / Chandigarh
Chennai / Ernakulam / Guwahati / Hyderabad / Jaipur
Lucknow / Mumbai / New Delhi / Patna

© Universities Press (India) Limited 2001

First published 2001
ISBN 81 7371 361 8

Typeset by
OSDATA
Hyderabad 500 029

Printed in India at
Baba Barkha Nath Printers
New Delhi

Published by
Universities Press (India) Limited
3-5-819 Hyderguda, Hyderabad 500 029

To
Partho and Amit
who encouraged me constantly

CONTENTS

Foreword   ix

Acknowledgements   xi

1. Branding   1
2. Brand Management   8
   New Product Development
   BOOST   8
   A New Product — An Excellent Concept, but Difficult to Substantiate
   MOTHER'S SPECIAL   20
3. Brand Positioning   29
   Introduction of an International Brand
   BACARDI   29
4. Brand Re-positioning   47
   KEO KARPIN HAIR OIL   47
   Smart Skincare
   KEO KARPIN BODY OIL   52
5. Creating Brands   54
   From Commodity to Branding
   Start of a Brand
   ARVIND'S ORIGINAL DENIM   58
   How a Company Converts a Commodity into a Brand
   GUJARAT AMBUJA CEMENT   63
   Diamonds as a Brand
   DE BEERS   69

6. Company / Product Branding   80
   The Story of Time in India
   TITAN   80

7. Power of Brand Equity — Brand Extension   94
   Brand Extension — the Real Winner
   MAGGI   96
   Brand Extension
   MAGGI KETCHUP & SAUCES   99
   Brand Extension — The Key to Volume Sale
   DETTOL   101
   DETTOL SOAP   103
   Horlicks Brand Extension
   ELAICHI HORLICKS   105
   HORLICKS BISCUITS   108
   Further Brand Extensions   110

8. Power of Branding   112
   Niche Marketing
   GENTEEL   112
   A New Brand Idea — Niche Marketing
   HAPPINESS   116
   Upgrading in a New Environment
   SUPER 777 BAR   121

9. Enhancing Brand Image through Promotions   129
   BOURNVITA Book of Knowledge   130
   BOOST Train Picture Cards   133

10. Protection of your Brand in a Competitive Environment   137
    HORLICKS vs. NESTOMALT   137

11. Brand Management   144
    Customer is the King: Will Always Be
    LIPTON'S YELLOW LABEL vs.
    BROOKE BOND'S RED LABEL   144

12. The Indian Experience   150

FOREWORD

"What is a brand?" Pran Choudhury starts his new book, *Successful Branding* with this rhetorical question. Pran provides a definition—"a brand is nothing but a way of creating an identity; almost like identifying a specific person within a large crowd." I have a different definition. My definition acknowledges the above definition and is also suitable when applied to all the brands mentioned in this book.

I believe that a brand is (or should be) a mark of pride and a simplifier of consumer choice. Hence, in my view a brand is the name of a marketable unit to which a unique, relevant and motivating set of associations and benefits, both functional and emotional, have become attached.

Understanding what a brand is and how to develop a strong brand lies at the heart of this publication. Pran Choudhury has collected a set of Indian case studies, which illustrate the principles of successful branding. The brands cover both Indian and foreign brand names and demonstrate all aspects of brand management from brand positioning (and re-positioning) to creating strong brands and the development of brand extension(s).

Many of the case studies reflect the author's personal involvement. Indeed, two of the case studies concern brands which I have had to compete with in the market place. Competing with such brands was a difficult, as well as an educative, experience for me. These two 'brand wars' demonstrated to me the skill and patience that Pran brought into the area of branding. I use the words 'skill' and 'patience' advisedly. These are two important characteristics of brand builders. First, brand builders must have the skills necessary to build brands. One of the objectives of this book is to illustrate the skills required for brand-building and a careful reading of the contents of this book will certainly help the reader in that area.

Secondly, brand-building requires patience. Brands are not built in a day or even in a year. The best known brands (or the strongest brands) in India are, as published annually by a leading Advertising and Marketing magazine, brands which have been in the market for thirty years or more, perhaps even half a century. So, while age, by itself is not a guarantee of a strong brand, most strong and successful brands in India and around the world have been present in the consumers' minds for several years. Brand-building efforts build the brand over a period of time.

There is a third important ingredient in the building of strong brands, and, this has not been touched upon in Pran Choudhury's book. The third important ingredient is *Luck,* on the part of the brand manufacturers. Inspite of considerable skill and investments there are many brands which do not succeed. I believe it is a question of having the right idea at the right time in the right circumstances, and then, doing the right things with the right amount of money at the right period of time. *In order to do all these things in the right way you must have the right amount of luck*. Case studies on marketing success rarely comment on this aspect.

This book will be of interest to both students and practitioners and can be read at leisure, or, with the intensity that characterise good marketing professionals. The principles stated in the book are global principles and it is most interesting to see them being applied in the Indian market place.

As we move into the 21st century, the importance of branding will increase significantly. This book will serve as a training manual, and will be an extremely useful guide for those involved in the difficult and challenging field of developing strong and profitable brands.

New Delhi   **Shunu Sen**
May 2000   CEO, Quadra Advisory
                                          [Former Group Marketing Adviser,
                                          Levers Group of Companies, India]

ACKNOWLEDGEMENTS

After the very encouraging response to my first book, *Successful Sales Promotion* — it was on the *Economic Times* best-sellers list for nine consecutive weeks — my colleagues and well-wishers have been urging me to write another book of the same type, i.e., based on Indian case studies. It has taken me almost eight years to come up with this second book. Collecting case study materials was not easy — it was occasionally tedious and sometimes frustrating — because you had to go, again and again, to the concerned companies for the relevant matter, as some of these cases were several years old. However, with the help of some of my erstwhile colleagues, as well as old and new business associates, I have been able to put together, what, I think, is a representative sample of very interesting and thought-provoking case studies on what is generally termed 'the Power of Brand Equity'.

For obvious reasons it is not possible to list the names of all those people and their companies who have helped me write this book. However, I would like to take this opportunity to thank some of those who have actively helped me, not only with the details of these case studies, but also with their general advice and suggestions. They are:

(1) Mr. Mike Khanna, H.T.A., Mumbai;
(2) Mr. Vijay (Java) Ramachandran, H.T.A., Mumbai;
(3) Mr. Sanjay Sehgal, Nestlé India Ltd., New Delhi;
(4) Mr. A.K. Tadanki, Nestlé India Ltd., New Delhi;
(5) Mr. Simon Scarff, SmithKline Beecham Consumer Healthcare, New Delhi;
(6) Mr. Nirvic Singh, Trikaya-Grey Advertising, Mumbai;
(7) Mr. Param Saikia, McCann Ericson, New Delhi;

(8) Mr. Kishore Chakraborty, McCann Ericson, Calcutta;
(9) Mr. Vivek Nayer, Reckitt and Colman India Ltd., New Delhi;
(10) Mr. Achin Ganguly, Ogilvy & Mather, New Delhi; and
(11) Mr. Nikhil Nehru, McCann Ericson, New Delhi.

In particular I would like to thank my old friend Rupen Bose, who provided a serene atmosphere at his house in Kasauli, where I wrote the bulk of the case studies. And of course the two young people — Simron and Sunil — who did all the typing.

One other point. Since I have been involved personally with some of the cases mentioned here, I have taken the liberty to use words like 'I' or 'we', while explaining a certain course of action. I have also taken the liberty of quoting two case studies from my earlier book *Successful Sales Promotion* under the heading "Enhancing Brand Image through Promotions".

And lastly, I do hope that the book will be both interesting and useful to practising Brand Managers, Account Service Managers of Advertising Agencies, who help the Marketing Companies to build brands; and to the students of Marketing who aspire to be Brand Managers.

Pran K. Choudhury

1

BRANDING

Introduction

What is a *brand*? It is nothing but a way of creating an identity for a product, somewhat like identifying a specific person within a large crowd. A quick example that comes to mind is that of Amitabh Bachchan whose name evokes a certain identity. When you think of Amitabh Bachchan you automatically identify him through certain characteristics and qualities which make him uniquely distinguishable from the many other stars. Or for that matter take the sun. There are millions of stars but when we talk of the sun, we immediately know which star we are referring to. Similarly, when we want to sell or buy a product, we do not think in terms of the product in general — we are required to identify the particular brand within the entire product range which we like. For example, when we go to buy a packet of tea, we do not ask for any packet of tea, we ask for a specific brand, i.e., Lipton's *Green Label* or Brooke Bond's *Red Label*.

Is it as simple as that? Of course not. It has taken a lot of time and effort to become the 'Big B' as we know him today. That is how a brand is built.

A brand is essentially the sum total of the particular satisfaction that it delivers to the consumer who buys that specific brand. This sum total relates in its entirety to its name, ingredients, price, packaging, distribution, reputation, and ultimately to its performance.

We, therefore, relate to brands. As consumers, we can remember some brands with which we are familiar and, therefore, we expect certain standards of quality from these brands. For example, when we want to buy a washing powder, we specifically ask for *Surf, Ariel* or some such brand.

Brand Equity

Brand Equity encompasses a set of assets linked to a brand's name and symbol that adds to the value provided by a product or service to a company's customers. There is always the underlying expectation that the brand will deliver the satisfaction it has promised. A consumer expects a certain standard of quality and the manufacturer has to make sure that the product lives up to that expectation, otherwise the consumer will stop buying the brand. Simply speaking, brand identities primarily exist in the minds of its consumers. A brand is his or her evaluation of the performance of that brand. And if this evaluation is positive the customer is willing to pay more for one particular brand over another similar product. This is the strength of Brand Equity.

You may well ask why there is such fascination with brands, and what are they worth? The reasons are many. Firstly, it is because brands create Trust, and trust is the basic precondition to Loyalty. Ultimately it is loyalty that ensures sustainable income to the companies that own these brands. It is this relationship, born out of loyalty, that ensures continuous sales, and therefore profit to the company. Secondly, it is because brands can be shown to be valuable to shareholders.

Once again, why is Brand Equity important? It is important because a strong Brand Equity enables the brand to command a premium. The reason customers are prepared to pay a premium is because of the perceived reliability, trustworthiness, as well as the positive image of superior quality that the brand commands. As emphasised, the major assets of Brand Equity can be categorised as:

(1) *Brand Awareness*: This refers to the strength of a brand's presence in the consumer's mind. Awareness is measured according to the recognition and recall of the brand.
(2) *Perceived Quality*: Perceived quality lies at the heart of what customers are buying; and in that sense, it is the ultimate measure of the impact of a brand.

(3) *Brand Loyalty*: A brand's value to the company is largely created by the customer loyalty it commands. Since a company considers loyalty as a major asset, it encourages and justifies loyalty building programmes which, in turn, helps create and enhance Brand Equity. In a way, the loyal customer gets emotionally attached to the brand.

Brands add value. In fact in one of the presentations made by Trikaya-Grey Advertising, it was called "The Value Focus Approach". I thought it was aptly presented, and I take the liberty to quote:

> Brands are built block-by-block and the best analogy one can give is how a building is constructed.
>
> The building of a brand is a three-part process. The first part relates to the idea. Like an Architect, the Marketing Manager must not only be able to visualise whether there is a consumer need for a particular product but also in what form. It is only when he has been able to pinpoint his particular need, that he can proceed further in terms of satisfying that need.
>
> This leads to the second part. Like construction of a building, he must have certain ingredients to build up the brand which will satisfy that need. For example, what should be the physical properties of the product? How is the brand going to be positioned? How will it look? What should its price be and so on. These are the inputs through which the brand is built.
>
> The third part relates to the process. In other words, all the ingredients we saw in the second part—how are we going to use these ingredients to make the brand? This process includes research, the logic behind the introduction of the brand, creativity in terms of how to project the brand to the consumer and of course, make sure there is adequate quality control to ensure that the product delivers what it promises.

This process is a continuous one. For any further stages of development, research has to be done to make sure that the brand is being developed along the right lines. When I said that a brand is built brick-by-brick, I meant that not only does it take time, — what is probably more important — it takes money and patience. Unfortunately, from my personal experience I am sorry to say that most of

THE VALUE FOCUS APPROACH

```
                    ┌───────────┐
                    │ MARKETING │
                    └─────┬─────┘
              ┌───────────┼───────────┐
              ▼           ▼           ▼
```

CHOOSE THE VALUE
- understand value desires
- select target
- define benefits / price

PROVIDE THE VALUE
- product development
- manufacture
- service
- price

COMMUNICATE THE VALUE
- sales message
- advertising / promotion

our aspiring industrialists are only traders: they want to see profit almost immediately. A fair amount of time and money is necessary to build a brand and very rarely does a brand become profitable before the first three introductory years are over. Naturally the brand loses money in the first two years, it may make some money in the third; but cumulatively it will still lose money in the third year. Indian businessmen, by and large, are not willing to absorb this loss or wait patiently for the fourth year. It is for this reason that, today, most of the successful brands in the market are owned by multinationals, barring of course a few like *Nirma, Titan,* etc.

Recently a mustard oil manufacturing company came to me for help in building a brand identity for their product as they wanted to get into consumer product marketing. A review of their current business confirmed that they not only had a good product, they also had a fair amount of acceptance among traders, and to a lesser extent, among consumers of a particular state. I, therefore, thought that with the right inputs we might be able to build the brand within two years. Since they had an ongoing business, my forecast indicated a fair amount of business for the branded product in the very first year, but investment of almost their entire profit (including trade business) in that year was also required. In other words, a no-profit, no-loss deal for the company was indicated for the first year. Forecast did indicate that in the second year, there would be a small profit; but the third year would definitely show substantial increase, both in business and profit.

After they had time to digest my forecast for the first three years, they came to the conclusion that they didn't want to get into the brand-building exercise. This was a great pity since I was confident they had a sure-fire winner in the so-called commodity market. In my opinion, most of our would-be industrialists (read businessmen) don't mind investing in machines and buildings, but they are very chary of investing in advertising and promotion, which is a must if you want to build a brand. Their argument goes somewhat like this: if at the end of the prescribed period you find you have made a mistake you at least have the building and the machinery to show for it, which will fetch a price in the open market. In short, you can see the tangible assets of your investment. On the other hand, all the money spent on advertising and promotion, has been irrecoverably spent, and there is nothing at all to tangibly show for it. How do you argue against such irrefutable logic!

Brand Identity—The Power of Mnemonic

One of the best ways of giving a distinctive identity to a brand is to formulate a suitable mnemonic. Over the years, this mnemonic becomes an inherent part of the brand name, due to continuous exposure, both in the media and on the packet itself. The importance of using mnemonic devices successfully has been explained in some of the case studies that will be discussed later in this book. However, I would like to recall one particular incident here which will exemplify the important role mnemonic can play in building a brand.

It happened in 1955 when I was working with Lipton, Madras. In those days (and I suppose even in these days), to a certain extent at least, the business was built on distribution and selling, rather than on advertising and promotion. Naturally a lot of time was spent in the field to monitor good distribution. As Assistant Branch Manager, I was in the field for almost fifteen days a month. During one such field visit in one of the smaller towns of Tamilnadu — I think it was near Tanjore — I was store-checking, when an elderly lady came to the shop and asked for a 20gm pack of Lipton's *Kora* dust tea. The fact that she had specifically asked for Lipton tea drew my attention. However, I also realised that the brand *Kora* belonged to Brooke Bond. Hence, my curiosity was further heightened. The shopkeeper took out a packet of Lipton's *Tea Girl* and gave it to the old lady. Both *Kora* and *Tea Girl* had yellow wrappers, but these were competitive brands. Her reaction was immediate — she did not want a packet of *Tea Girl* tea. When the shopkeeper explained that since she had asked for Lipton's dust tea, he had given her *Tea Girl* tea, which is what Lipton produces. However, the lady was quite clear as to what she wanted — she wanted the packet which had a picture of "mother and child". *Kora* packets did have pictures of a mother and child (almost like Virgin Mary and child) as a mnemonic. When the shopkeeper showed her a packet of *Kora*, the lady smiled and confirmed that that was indeed the tea she had wanted all along. The shopkeeper then explained to her that this was Brooke Bond tea and not Lipton, which was actually what she had wrongly asked for, by name. The lady was quite sure that what she wanted was *Kora* tea (with mother and child mnemonic), the company name, Lipton or Brooke Bond, had never really mattered to her.

To me, this whole incident demonstrated the power of easily recognisable mnemonic as an important part of branding. Sure, the brand name is important; but in a society where illiteracy is still quite prevalent (especially in rural and semi-urban areas), mnemonic will continue to play a very important role in the brand-building and marketing of consumer products, such as tea, which has its franchise in the smaller towns and villages.

2

BRAND MANAGEMENT

New Product Development

BOOST

Until 1975, HMM (now SmithKline Beecham Consumer Healthcare) was known as a single product company, namely *Horlicks*. It was due to its technical and marketing strength in the Malted Milkfood Market that HMM management took a decision to enter the brown powder segment in 1972. In order to appreciate HMM's decision, it would be necessary to take a look at this market.

Malted Milkfood Market

The Malted Milkfood Market in India is divided into two segments — white and brown powders. In 1972, the white powder segment contributed 61 per cent of the total market, and brown, the balance of 39 per cent. Traditionally, the white powder business was concentrated in the Southern and Eastern regions where milk supply was either inadequate and/or of doubtful quality. On the other hand, brown powders were distributed throughout the country, but the Southern region dominated the market with 50 per cent of the brown powder business. The Eastern region's share was rather low.

In 1972, the total MFD (milkfood) market was 15,000 tons and was growing at the rate of 5 per cent. All brown powder products claimed cocoa or chocolate as their main ingredient and they were used mainly as milk additives to make milk tastier and therefore, more palatable.

When HMM decided to enter the brown powder segment, there were two main competitors, *Bournvita* and *Ovaltine*, and their share of business was as follows:

   Bournvita – 75%
   Ovaltine   – 18%
   Others   – 7%

When the New Product Development Committee of HMM met in April 1972 for finalising a product brief, Technical pointed out two constraints. They were:

(1) The Malted Milkfood license which authorised HMM to manufacture milkfood products stipulated that the product must contain 7.5 per cent of animal fat, which meant that a minimum quantity of milk had to be used. (*Bournvita*, the product category leader, did not have this constraint and in fact, was using only 5 per cent of animal fat as they operated under a different license.)

(2) Cocoa needed to be imported and since HMM had no import license, HMM would have to buy it at a higher cost apart from the fact that HMM would find it very difficult to obtain cocoa in large quantities.

Product brief

In July 1972 a product brief was prepared, the salient points of which were:

(1) The product should have a distinctive taste to suit the Indian palate. In other words, it must not be a "me too" product.
(2) The quantity of cocoa to be used should be minimal, without in any way, reducing the cocoa flavour and taste *vis-à-vis Bournvita*, the brand leader.
(3) No sugar could be added as that would mean contravening the license requirements under which HMM manufactures malted milkfood.

(4) The product should be granular and look like any other brown milkfood powder.
(5) The end price should be equal to the brand leader, i.e., *Bournvita*.

Product development

On the basis of the product brief, HMM's Technical Department began developing a brown milkfood, and in April 1973 developed two flavour variants — HC44 and HC3.

Basically HC44 was made up of malt extracts whereas HC3 had *Horlicks* as the main ingredient. These were then handed over to the Indian Market Research Bureau (IMRB) for conducting a blind in-hall, round robin test in June 1973. The two variants were tested along with *Bournvita* and *Ovaltine*.

The top-line results of this test indicated a preference for HC44 over HC3. The former variant was also preferred to *Ovaltine*, but lost out to *Bournvita*. In other words, the preferred variant (HC44) fell somewhere between *Bournvita* and *Ovaltine*, the two competing brands. However, on individual attribute ratings, it was found that there were a number of contradictions. Therefore it was decided, in September 1973, that both the variants HC44 and HC3 would be tested in an in-home situation, along with *Bournvita* and *Ovaltine*. The products were placed sequentially, in order to eliminate the possibility of recognition of the usual product. As a further precaution, *Bournvita* and *Ovaltine* were sieved to give an appearance similar to that of HC44 and HC3. The regularly used product was removed from the home.

This test was conducted in the two metros, Chennai and Mumbai, using a much larger sample than in the June 1973 research. Each of the two flavour variants, HC44 and HC3, were thus tested in-home against *Bournvita* and *Ovaltine*. In addition, these two variants were tested against each other among *Bournvita* and *Ovaltine* users. It was clear from the above tests that:

(1) HC44 was clearly the better of the two formulations (which, incidentally, was also the result of the earlier in-hall test).

(2) Both *Bournvita* and *Ovaltine* were preferred to HC44 among both adults and children.

The survey also indicated that the most important dimensions determining preference for a drink were taste, flavour (particularly a chocolate flavour) and sweetness levels. On the basis of these three dimensions consumers felt that:

(1) both HC44 and HC3 should have a stronger chocolate flavour;
(2) the bitter/medicinal taste in the two variants should be eliminated; and
(3) both variants should be made sweeter.

Technical was briefed accordingly to improve upon HC44. In July 1974, Technical produced two improved varieties of HC44 which were then subjected to in-company tests. As one of the two variants did well against *Ovaltine*, but not so against the brand leader *Bournvita*, that product was placed for in-home, in-company tests with known *Bournvita* users. The result was encouraging (30 per cent preferred HC44), although *Bournvita* was still preferred by the majority of the users.

When the result of this in-company research was discussed by the Development Committee, Technical pointed out that given the constraints, namely minimum use of cocoa, non-use of sugar, and at the same time more use of animal fat, it would be difficult to further improve on the three dimensions indicated earlier, i.e., taste, flavour and sweetness. On the other hand, the in-home, in-company test did confirm that the improved HC44 had a distinct flavour and taste of its own.

In November 1974, after a period of two-and-a-half years from the date the product brief was given, HMM Management decided to test launch the product (rather than go for another product test) in order to find out its acceptance under real market conditions.

However, before we discuss the test launch, let us look at the other activities that were happening simultaneously with product development.

Packaging

The original product brief, of July 1972, had recommended that the product should be packed in a glass jar for the following reasons:

(1) The glass jar would give a distinctive product image, as all existing brown powders were being marketed in tins.
(2) In India, after-use of a container is a very strong selling point for a housewife.
(3) Costwise, a glass jar would be cheaper than a tin.
(4) There were a variety of shapes available in glass.
(5) It was stressed that the mouth of the glass jar should be wide enough for a housewife to put her hand inside the jar so that its after-use value is enhanced.

Technical produced a wooden mock-up in consultation with one of the Indian glass bottle manufacturers in February 1974. The salient features of the mock-up were:

(1) The size of the mouth took an 88mm cap – the biggest ever produced in India at that time.
(2) There would be rings, both at the top and the bottom, as a result of which, if there was any ullage at the top, it would not be noticed easily by the customer.

Technical also confirmed that when produced, the bottle would become the largest bottle ever manufactured in India on automatic machinery. The sample glass bottle was approved by the Development Committee at their meeting held in July 1974.

Brand name

While development on the product and its container were still on, HMM worked in close collaboration with its advertising agency – HTA, in order to select a brand name suitable for the product. A list of names were selected for pre-testing and IMRB was briefed accordingly in August 1973. The test was conducted in a total sample size of 400: Mumbai – 100, Delhi – 100 and Chennai – 200.

In December 1973, IMRB submitted their report. The 9 selected names were ranked in terms of respondents' overall preference and

their views on suitability for a brown MFD. A ranking of 1 would indicate the most liked/suitable name, while a rank of 9 would represent the least liked/suitable name. A summary of the name test results can be seen in Table 2.1.

Table 2.1 *Summary of Name Test Results*

Names tested	Overall preference	Suitability for a brown milkfood
Boost	1	2
Brownie	3	4
Bruno	4	3
Revenaq	8	6
Solo	7	5
Tango	6	7
Tiger	5	8
Vita-Plus	2	1
Zip	9	9

On the basis of this result, HMM therefore selected the name *Boost* for the new product.

Label and logo design

Once the brand name was selected, HMM decided to commission the National Institute of Design (NID), Ahmedabad, to help produce the necessary label and logo design. The Institute was briefed accordingly in February 1974, and was requested to present its final recommendations by October 1974. NID made three presentations. During the first presentation in June 1974, HMM pointed out that whereas the Institute had been able to put across the mood of the brand name, the visibility, as well as the readability, of the brand name was not very good. At the second presentation in August 1974, it was found that although the logo design had improved considerably in all other respects, it was still not fully readable from a distance, particularly, if the bottle was kept on a slightly dark shelf. It was at this stage that HMM Management decided that the words "From the Makers of *Horlicks*" should also be incorporated on the label.

The final presentation was made in October 1974. At this stage, HMM worked in close collaboration with HTA, who put the finishing touches on the label design. The final label was then approved by the Development Committee at its meeting in November 1974. Let us now take a look at how the advertising for *Boost* was developed.

Advertising Campaign

In the advertising brief that was handed over to the advertising agency, HTA, in early '74, HMM stressed the following points:

(1) As past research had shown, brown powders were generally used as milk additives to make milk tastier. The main target consumers would be children who, traditionally, have been given milk to drink by Indian mothers.

(2) Since all brands in the malted milkfood market (both white and brown) were virtually claiming the same end benefits, namely energy/strength and nourishment, the campaign would have to try and project some unique feature of the product, which provided specific benefits so as to distinguish it from other products.

(3) As *Horlicks* was by far the brand leader and also HMM's only line of business, the new product's claim should not clash in any way with the claims of *Horlicks* and thus maybe, eat into the sales of *Horlicks*. In other words, the campaign had to be distinctly different from the *Horlicks* campaign.

While HTA was working on this campaign, the London office of Beecham's was working with J.Walter Thompson, London. The creative director at JWT, while presenting his ideas for the campaign said:

> "Taking into account the fact that there could be any analogy between the fuel needed by a steam engine and the energy-giving food needed by a growing child, I have tried to bring a link between the two types of energy so as to make it visually attractive and memorable."

However, the difficulty arose in trying to develop a visual which would depict a railway engine — and then tie it up with a beverage. Somehow, the two did not seem to aesthetically blend. Here, HTA

Now! Get the energy fuel for an active life.

Boost
MALT CHOCOLATE MILK DRINK.

Like a train, you also need the fuel to get to a good start every day. That's why you need BOOST every morning.

Energy fuel that helps keep you going at top speed. Especially your children, who use up extra energy at work and play.

Give them BOOST, the malt chocolate milk drink. From the makers of 'Horlicks', the people who know all about nourishment.

Rich creamy Boost gives you more energy because it is made from whole-cream milk, wheat, barley malt and cocoa.

Boost contains more nutritious ingredients than any other similar chocolatey drink for your childrens' growth.

And BOOST has that delicious, creamy malt chocolate flavour your whole family will love.

BOOST. It's the perfect way to start your day. Every day.

Available in two sizes.

From the makers of 'Horlicks.'

India came up with a solution. They suggested the use of the words "Energy Fuel" and showed a train with a bottle of *Boost* as the passenger.

When this campaign was discussed by HTA with HMM, the consensus of opinion was that although the concept of the train engine was a good one, somehow, the absence of a human element made the layout rather unattractive. It was at this stage that the Creative Director of HTA found a solution. It would be interesting to go into the details of this creative process. He said: "On a Sunday morning, while sitting in my room, I saw young children playing games and they had formed what could be called a 'human' train. They started jogging and began to make the typical chugging noise of a train. It then struck me that if I could portray this human train along with a railway train with engine, I would be able to establish the relationship between the two, much more effectively. At the same time, I would have our target group form an integral part of the campaign." The result is for all to see now.

Test launch

HMM Management decided to test launch the product initially in just one state, and selected Kerala for it. Kerala, one of the southern states, was selected for the test launch for the following reasons:

(1) Kerala test market results could be extrapolated for the entire south, which represented 50 per cent of the brown powder volume.
(2) Being a strong *Horlicks* market, the test market would help identify whether there would be cannibalisation (this was important because profit on *Boost* should ideally be less than on *Horlicks*).
(3) Being a compact state, there should be negligible outflow of stocks or media inputs.
(4) High local mass media availability would help spread the advertising message quickly and effectively.
(5) High literacy levels, combined with high consumer consciousness would enable quicker feedback, both on the product and on advertising. Remember, there was no TV channel available for advertising at that time.

Boost was thus finally launched on 9 May 1975, (three years from the date of the product brief) in Kerala at the same price as *Bournvita*. It received the following marketing inputs during the launch.

Marketing inputs — Kerala

(1) Local excitement was created through processions of elephants announcing the introduction of *Boost*.
(2) Liquid sampling of *Boost* was conducted in various offices/institutions as well as in-store.
(3) A trade deal of one 450gm bottle free with every case (containing 18 bottles) was offered.
(4) Display contests were conducted at selected outlets.

Media inputs

While press and cinema were used as primary media, (TV was not commercial at that time), radio and hoardings were used as secondary media.

Let us now look at the most important aspect of marketing.

Consumer offtake

ORG consumer offtake results (Nielson's shop audit equivalent in India) were available at the end of December 1975, i.e., 8 months after its introduction. Brand shares in the brown powder segment were as follows:

Bournvita	– 49%
Ovaltine	– 8%
Boost	– 40%
Others	– 3%

As can be seen *Boost* fared exceedingly well — from 0 to 40 per cent of the market.

Advertising research

An advertising post-test was carried out in December 1975, in two Class I towns and one Class II town in Kerala, among a total of 939 households. The main findings of the research were as follows:

(1) Over 90 per cent of the housewives contacted in each city had heard of *Boost*.
(2) The major sources of advertising recall were: newspapers (59%), radio (42%), cinema (24%) and shop displays (21%).
(3) Trial of *Boost* was remarkably high in all three cities — approximately 60 per cent. Currently, usage was roughly over half that of trial, i.e., 40 per cent.
(4) *Boost* appeared to have been adopted as a family drink, used equally by the housewife, her husband and the children.
(5) *Boost* was taken most often 'before going to bed' – 49%, 'at breakfast time' – 38%, and 'before going to work/school, etc,' – 23%.
(6) Current *Boost* users who were previously *Bournvita* or *Ovaltine* users, felt that the brand was slightly better than *Bournvita / Ovaltine*, particularly in terms of taste, children's preference and miscibility.
(7) Among current *Boost* users, the greatest proportion had switched either from *Bournvita* (43%), or *Horlicks* (29%).
(8) 96 per cent of the respondents served or drank *Boost* daily.
(9) The bottle and overall packaging of *Boost* was liked by most housewives; as many as 23 per cent of *Boost* triers said that the bottle was an important factor in influencing purchase of the brand.
(10) The fact that *Boost* is manufactured by the makers of *Horlicks* did not seem to be a factor influencing brand trial or usage.

Conclusion

After the successful 'test marketing' of *Boost*, the brand was rolled out to the rest of India — first in the South, then in the East, and subsequently in the North and West.

Today, it is the second largest brand of SmithKline Beecham's Consumer Healthcare Company, producing an annual sale of rupees 80 crores, and still growing. It is also the number 2 brand, after

Bournvita, in the brown powder segment. However, the brand took four years to be cumulatively profitable — a lesson all brand managers must be alive to.

Postscript

When I first presented the *Boost* campaign to my boss in London, he and his team appreciated the analogy between the steam locomotive engine with coal as fuel, and *Boost* giving vital energy to the children to sustain their energy. However, they objected to the word 'fuel' and to the slug line:

Energy fuel for an active life

They wondered how 'fuel' could be consumed or eaten! To them fuel was something that could not be consumed and therefore the campaign needed to be changed.

Initially I tried to explain that in India, it would not be misunderstood as we were familiar with what is known as 'Indian English'; and in that context it would not create any dissonance. Unfortunately this explanation did not satisfy them. Since I was very keen to get the campaign accepted (as all of us in India felt that the campaign would definitely be a winner), I had to fall back on an old cliché. I said that, since more than 50 per cent of the market (brown MFD market, as we define it) was in South India, and as most of the advertising needed to be done in the local language, the slug line would give the right meaning in the context of that language. I knew that it would be very difficult for them to challenge such a statement. Even then, I found them rather reluctant to give in to the campaign. The decision was deferred to the next day. The idea was to call in the advertising agency (JWT in this case) to see if a better campaign could be worked out — more or less on the same theme.

I went back to the hotel, a bit disappointed. Having slept over the matter, the next morning I made a statement right at the beginning of the meeting which, fortunately for me (as it turned out) resulted in far-reaching consequences. I said that I was prepared to accept any change that London might suggest and also implement the same wholeheartedly with my team, but I would not accept responsibility for the result. If, on the other hand, London accepted the campaign *in toto*, the responsibility would be entirely mine, and if it did not produce the desired results, they could have my neck. For a moment there was pindrop silence. My boss, who was the MD of the International Division tried to carry the discussion further in order to come to some sort of consensus. But, I stuck to my guns, without being obviously belligerent. Ultimately they gave in, taking into account the fact that in a local language the slug line would be much more acceptable given the fact that most of the ad would anyway be in the local language.

Mother's Special

Breast-feeding is best for your baby's health. Breast milk is the best and purest food for your baby. It is also very easy to digest, so your baby stays free from stomach troubles. Moreover, it helps to build up his resistance to illness. That is why it is advisable for you to feed your baby for as long as you can.

Why you need 'Mother's Special'? When you are breast-feeding, you are passing on the nutrition from your body to your baby. That is why international experts in the World Health Organisation state that mothers need additional nutrition when they are breast feeding.

'Mother's Special' is a unique formulation that helps to ensure you get your additional requirements of calories, proteins, vitamins, calcium, iron and other nutrients, as recommended by these experts.

Directions

To make a nourishing drink, take 21 gms. (2 heaped teaspoons) of powder in 200 ml. (one glass) hot milk. The milk should not be boiling. Add sugar as required. For maximum benefit take it twice a day.

Mother's Special

The health drink for breast-feeding mothers.

From the makers of **Horlicks**

MADE IN INDIA BY
H M M
LIMITED
NABHA, PUNJAB

under licence from

HORLICKS LIMITED
BRENTFORD
MIDDLESEX, U.K.

NET WEIGHT
500 GMS

FREE SAMPLE
NOT FOR SALE

A New Product — An Excellent Concept, but Difficult to Substantiate

MOTHER'S SPECIAL

Background

In one of the meetings of the New Product Development Committee of HMM (now SmithKline Beecham Healthcare), way back in 1976, it was agreed to try and capitalise on the main strengths of the company. These were:

(1) Brand equity of *Horlicks*;
(2) The company's image as a manufacturer of high quality health products;
(3) Very satisfactory equation with the medical profession, which has been recommending *Horlicks* for almost half a century;
(4) The faith housewives have in the 'do good' ability of *Horlicks*; and
(5) The knowledge and expertise that Technical had developed and acquired in the field of milk-based products.

Based on the premise that, "breastfeeding mothers need additional nutrition", HMM proposed in April 1976, that a dietary supplement product specially designed to meet the nutritional requirements of nursing mothers should be created.

Concept

A dietary supplement for breastfeeding mothers which would help ensure that the mother is able to provide her baby with sufficient quantity, and satisfactory quality of breast milk. Since the company was entering into an area where there was no published data available in terms of total market, or the consumer's attitude and beliefs towards breastfeeding, the company first decided to carry out research in two stages.

Research

Stage 1 would be a quantitative survey amongst breastfeeding mothers to help define the market structure and provide the basis for sales projections. The main findings of this Stage 1 research were:

(1) Over 90 per cent of mothers do breastfeed their children.
(2) In the majority of cases the bottle has been introduced between the age of 1 to 3 months.
(3) By the age of 6 months all children were being bottle fed either exclusively or in combination with the breast.

On the basis of these findings the company was able to prepare the regionwise market size.

In Stage 2 research, the company tried to find the answer to the following questions:

(1) attitudes and beliefs regarding breastfeeding;
(2) which segment, i.e., exclusive breastfeeding, a combination of bottle and breastfeeding, or exclusive bottle-feeding would present the maximum potential for the new product; and
(3) which would be the best approach for communicating the benefits of this product. In other words, evaluating alternative product concepts.

The main findings of this Stage 2 research were:

(1) The two groups: exclusively breastfeeding mothers, and the group with a combination of breast and bottle would form the primary target group.
(2) Whereas the quantity improvement is a credible claim, the quality improvement claim could face a credibility problem.
(3) Both 'Caring Mother' and 'Nature Care' communication approaches had been well-received.
(4) Breast milk and breastfeeding was always considered supreme.
(5) Mothers liked the idea that the product was a health drink, and not a medicine.

Product proposition

The product was made from wheat, malted barley, milk fat and added vitamins. When combined with milk this formula would provide 100 per cent of additional proteins and vitamins and 82 per cent of the additional calories required by breastfeeding mothers, as recommended by WHO. The company checked these details with R&D and Technical. Both agreed to the claim. Further, the product would be recommended by doctors. Above all, the product was made by the makers of *Horlicks*, who knew all about nourishment.

To derive the full benefit of the product it would be recommended that the product be drunk twice a day; each drink containing 20gm of the product dissolved in 200ml of standard milk. Generally Indian nursing mothers drank milk twice a day. The feedback from consumer trials was very favourable.

Brand name

As far as brand name was concerned, the company researched 12 alternative brand names and 'Mother's Special' came out the clear winner. During the initial research conducted by the company 'Caring Mother' and 'Nature Care' was considered the best but these brand names did not exactly convey what was meant to be communicated.

There was another important point. Since the selected brand name specifically spelt out for whom the product was meant the danger of giving this product to the baby was minimal. This was important, since during one of the meetings with quasi-government authorities it became clear that if the company was not careful, mothers might use the product as a substitute for baby food; and that would be disastrous. Therefore, it was essential that the label make it very clear that the product was meant only for mothers. It was also agreed that using the brand name in association with *Horlicks* to create consumer trust and confidence, would be a good idea.

Packaging

The company preferred an amber coloured glass jar for maximum protection, and since by the very nature of the product it needed to be used for a minimum number of days in order to visibly realise the effect of the product, a 500gm size was selected.

As far as the label design was concerned, the design clearly indicated that the product was meant for breastfeeding mothers and the visual of mother and child further enhanced the emotive appeal.

Further research

Having completed product development the company then did the Stage 3 research: a full-fledged concept-cum-usage test with the complete product, namely, bottle, label, cap, etc.

The company also showed target consumers the format of the proposed press advertisement and got their views about the price at which the product would be marketed.

Research during usage of the product

The nursing mother would be contacted twice during her usage of the product—once after the product had been used for 10 days, the second time after the product had been used for approximately one month. The company particularly wanted to know, apart from the overall rating of the product, whether there was any flavour fatigue.

The results were very encouraging indeed. Approximately 70 per cent of the consumers felt that the product did increase the quantity of the breast milk. But what was probably more important was that they felt much more healthy after using it. As was expected, only about 50 per cent felt that the quality of the breast milk had improved. In any case how was she to find out! As far as the product attributes were concerned, it was favourable on all counts except on miscibility. Reaction to the advertisement was also favourable in so far as the respondent was able to comprehend that the product did increase the quantity of breast milk, and that it provided additional nutrition to breastfeeding mothers.

However, on two counts the communication did not appear to have done its job properly:

(1) that the product improved the quality of breast milk; and,

(2) that the product was recommended by doctors.

Since through Stage 2 research findings, the company knew that the claim of 'Quality Improvement' was suspect, it was decided not to strengthen this claim. The response to the visual was overwhelmingly favourable. On the other hand, as far as 'Recommended by Doctors' is concerned, (that being a very important part of the campaign), the advertisement did need strengthening, and accordingly doctors' endorsements were highlighted in a panel.

Test marketing

The company selected the metro Chennai, since, not only was it a strong *Horlicks* market but HMM also had very good rapport with the medical professionals there, whose support and backing the company felt the product certainly needed if it wanted to be successful in the market place.

The company decided to have a 12-months test period since the company was dealing with a mobile audience, and needed a period of 12 months to validate the assumptions across a representative sample.

Medical detailing

The company believed that for a product of this nature, given the background of Indian culture and habits, very few nursing mothers would try it unless it was recommended by a doctor or by a family friend. It is for this reason that the company felt that a very strong base had to be established, with the help of the medical profession, before it could be placed in the market. The company, therefore, planned to have four months of solus medical promotion before releasing it to the media.

The company proposed to cover broadly 50 per cent of the general doctor population, and 100 per cent of the gynaecologists and pediatricians. Similarly, it would cover almost all the maternity homes and wards.

In order to help the company's medical detailing team a detailing folder was prepared. This was prepared in such a way that a slightly different emphasis could be given while detailing to either gynaecologists or to pediatricians. The company also proposed to sample out the product and the advantage here was that the doctor was bound to dole out the product to some patient or the other, as distinct from using it in his own home. An attractive information folder giving all details about the product composition, etc., was left behind with the doctor for his reference.

Nursing home promotion

The company planned a special nursing home promotion whereby 1500 mothers with new-born babies would be contacted while they were still in maternity homes. The company felt that this was important because it initiated use of the product at the earliest date, and since it was being promoted in the nursing homes it would naturally enjoy the implied doctor's endorsement.

To further boost this kind of promotion the company also supplied a booklet on breastfeeding together with three discount coupons of Rs. 2/- each. The idea was that if she used three bottles she was bound to see the difference and therefore would continue to use the product. An attractive poster was hung in all the important nursing homes and clinics. Consumer service cards which would record the child's growth, was distributed free to all mothers through their doctors.

Mass media advertising

Media activity, therefore, was divided into two phases. The first phase, i.e., the first four months were kept exclusively for medical promotion. During the second phase mass media advertising was resorted to, but medical detailing continued.

Looking at the various media available at Chennai, the company felt that cinema was not appropriate; although television would have been an ideal media, because of the very limited number of sets in use at Chennai at that time, exposure would be rather limited. Hence, press coverage was selected as the primary media where it was possible to tell a long story convincingly. The company preferred weeklies since it had retention value and also because it catered to the target group. Radio was used as a reminder media, not through straight jingles or spots, but through sponsored programmes.

Distribution

Since at first the company was promoting the product only through the doctors, the initial distribution of the product would also be restricted to chemists' outlets. Gradually as mass media expanded the user base, the product distribution would be extended to general stores and grocery outlets. At that stage the company would use POS and other merchandising materials.

Need for continuous research

As it was a new concept and an entirely new product, it was absolutely essential that at every stage the company conduct research to validate the original assumptions regarding penetration, period of use, quantum consumed, etc. Similarly, feedback information, from the doctors and chemists as to what extent of support the company was getting from this important sector, was considered essential.

Brand Performance

Mother's Special was finally launched in the metro, Chennai, in October, 1980. It was retailed initially through chemists' and druggists' outlets, and supported through medical detailing. Later on, when the product was supported by mass media, mainly press and then by TV, the distribution was mainly extended to A class outlets.

In terms of overall sales performance, *Mother's Special* did better than budget; and what was probably more important, secondary sales were close to primary sales, thus reconfirming the company's correct communication and promotional strategy. Through a panel research conducted during the test marketing operation, it was noticed that gynaecologists/obstetricians were the single biggest source for initial awareness. Furthermore, nursing home sampling also turned out to be a winner — sales to sampling ratio was 1:3:4. A very high ratio indeed! The most gratifying feature however, was the support the brand received from doctors. Some of these doctors even congratulated HMM for taking the lead in introducing such a much-needed product.

The brand was extended to the rest of Tamilnadu and Calcutta in 1981, and then to Karnataka in 1982. In 1988/89, the brand was extended to the remaining parts of West Bengal, and the South, also to the North and Nepal. Unfortunately sales never took off, particularly in terms of volume. While analysing the not-so-satisfactory results, it was evident that:

(1) *Mother's Special* would never be a big selling brand, since its usage would always be for a limited period for a particular consumer.

(2) The customer base therefore, would always be a shifting one. In other words, loyal customers could be loyal only for a brief period. This cuts across the basic philosophy of the ever-growing volume business, which in effect, is the core advantage of brand loyalty.

(3) To recruit new consumers on an on-going basis, the company needed to spend continuously for advertising and promotional activities — a costly proposition, especially if the volume did not justify it. Also the product would need the support of the medical detailing team on a continuous basis, again a costly operation.

(4) To give credibility to the claim, 'Help improve quality of breast milk', the company must do, what is known in pharmaceutical parlance as, 'a clinical study', which is both expensive and time-consuming. Such an expenditure may not be justifiable if the volume was not going to support it.

As a result, a very good concept failed to translate into a credible, very good brand.

3

BRAND POSITIONING

Introduction of an International Brand

BACARDI

Background

The spirits market in India is still at an evolutionary stage and has only just emerged from being a regulated market, with very few established local players. Indian consumers have not had anywhere near the kind of choice available in the developed markets of the world. India has traditionally been a brown spirit market, which meant that rum and whisky have been the dominant product categories, with brandy claiming some limited share as well. Until a few years ago, white spirits, wines, liqueurs, cognacs, etc., were only present in upper end niche markets and all put together, were negligible in comparison to browns. This situation was common in many parts of the world as well — but twenty years ago. Those markets have since developed and white spirits now hold strong category shares.

Under the impact of the economic and cultural liberalisation policies that were put into effect in India during the early '90s, the spirits industry also saw a gradual shift towards white spirits and light-hearted drinking, away from the traditionally serious brown spirits.

As in other parts of the world, white spirits are gaining importance. It is this opportunity that Bacardi-Martini identified, and then, took a conscious decision to make their entry into India.

Market description

The following figures will give details of market situation at the time of the *Bacardi* launch in India, particularly the relationship between brown and white spirits. It also gives the future trend of development as envisaged by Bacardi.

Table 3.1 IMFL Market – Brown and White Spirits (9Ltr Cases in '000)

	Brown	White	Total
1985	15,000	750	15,750
1990	27,000	1,750	28,750
1995	47,000	2,300	49,300
2000	70,000	5,800	75,800
2005	100,000	10,000	110,000

Table 3.2 Brown & White Spirits: Progression Rate

	Brown	White
1995	94%	6%
2005	92%	8%

White Spirits in Greater Detail

The only major international white spirit brand in India at that time was *Smirnoff* vodka. Local brands, such as *Karmazov* and *Romanov*, had been around before that but were extreme niche brands and had no pan-Indian presence. Apart from vodka, gin was the other white spirit present in the market with *Blue Riband* being the only major player. In effect, white spirits were a nascent category. Attitudes to white spirits reflected some key problem areas:

* Whites are often seen as softer spirits, without the strength and punch of mainline liquor, such as whisky and rum.
* White spirits are also directly linked to femininity (e.g., "gin is a woman's drink").

* In terms of drinking occasions, white spirits were/are seen to fit into the daytime period, i.e., for an afternoon drink (pink gins at lunch?). This potentially limits consumption and thus volume sale.
* Research clearly showed category associations to be with — 'smooth, light-bodied', mixed with lime/orange, 'summers', afternoon', 'women', etc.

Research

Among the several market researches commissioned by Bacardi-Martini India Ltd., two were particularly useful: Concept Testing and a Usage & Attitude Study. These are outlined below.

Concept testing

Generally, the first stage in the development, positioning and communication of a brand involved the creation of certain brand concepts, which then had to be tested on the consumer. Therefore, Bacardi developed six concepts for this purpose, (detailed below), that were felt to have a relevance to both the brand, and to the motivations of the Indian consumer. The qualitative research was conducted at metropolitan centres across India; the method used was of exposing a focus group comprising likely future consumers to each concept and then eliciting their reactions on the same. To make the concepts lifelike, *concept cards* and *mood boards* were used.

---------------------------------| Concept 1 |---------------------------------

Introducing *Bacardi* rum

"Get Away To A Relaxed Carefree World"

Your daily life is full of pressures. This daily buzz of activity can take its toll on you. In fact there are times when you just want to get away from it all

Welcome to the World of Bacardi. A world of blue skies, white beaches, sea breeze and warm sunshine. Time stops moving while you do the things you enjoy — savouring the afternoon sun, lying on a hammock between gently swaying palms or playing beach ball with friends.

Bacardi rum is so smooth and clear that it blends with anything to give you a great refreshing taste. It tastes great with *Coke*, lemonade or simply 'on the rocks' with a slice of lime. Nothing is as cool as drifting in the sun, sipping on *Bacardi*.

Bacardi rum - Get Away To A Relaxed Carefree World.
Founded in Cuba in 1862.
Bacardi rum is available in a 750ml bottle. Price Rs. 300/-

Concept 2

Introducing *Bacardi* rum

"Experience the Spirit of Free Thinking"

Since 1862, *Bacardi* has been the favourite drink of free spirited people the world over. People who drink *Bacardi* are independent minded; they like to do their own thing and love the challenge of new situations. Their unpretentious nature, casual style and wit sets them apart from their peers.

They enjoy *Bacardi*, either on the rocks, with *Coke* or with anything that captures their imagination. *Bacardi* is a smooth, clear spirit that is remarkably easy to drink. In a world of dark spirits, the freshness of Bacardi symbolises the spirit of free thinking.

Bacardi rum - Experience the Spirit of Free Thinking.
Founded in Cuba in 1862.
Bacardi rum is available in a 750ml bottle. Price Rs. 300/-

Concept 3

Introducing *Bacardi* rum

"Feel the Cuban Passion"

In Cuba, people have a zest and passion for living life to the fullest, enjoying all the good things in life: friends, food, drink and music. Their music — sensual, rhythmic, with an infectious beat that makes you want to dance. Their drink — *Bacardi* rum, founded in Cuba in 1862.

Bacardi is so smooth and clear that it blends with anything. To refresh and tingle your senses try it with tonic, juice or simply on the rocks with a slice of lime. The all-time favourite of course is *Bacardi* & *Coca-Cola*. Drink *Bacardi* anyway you want it and unleash the Cuban spirit in you.

Bacardi rum - the Cuban Passion since 1862.

Bacardi rum is available in a 750ml bottle. Price Rs. 300/-

Concept 4

Introducing *Bacardi* rum.

"The World's Finest Rum since 1862"

Over a century ago, when rum was unrefined and often harsh, Don Facundo Bacardi, created in Cuba the world's first smooth, clear rum. Since 1862, Bacardi is made with the original refined formula that Don Facundo personally enjoyed. By blending special rums, charcoal filtered for smoothness and matured in oak barrels. The result — an exceptionally smooth, refined product with a subtle yet distinctive taste.

Bacardi is so smooth and clear — its mellow taste comes through beautifully, on the rocks, with a slice of lime, tonic or cola. In fact the world's most popular mixed drink is *Bacardi* & *Coca-Cola*, invented in Cuba in 1898 by an American soldier who mixed the two together.

Bacardi rum - the World's Finest Rum since 1862.

Bacardi rum is available in a 750ml bottle. Price Rs. 300/-

Concept 5

Introducing *Bacardi* rum

"The Spirit of Cuba since 1862"

In Cuba, people are warm, friendly and unpretentious. Willing to open their hearts and homes to friend and stranger alike, they love to share their good food and drink with those they welcome. They are very particular about the drink they serve, for they want only the best for themselves and their friends.

Bacardi, founded in Cuba in 1862, is the drink Cubans most enjoy. They like *Bacardi*'s clear smooth taste — a result of charcoal filtering and maturing in oak barrels — the same way it was made over a 100 years ago. They drink *Bacardi* simply on the rocks with a slice of lime, or *Coca-Cola*.

Bacardi rum - the Spirit of Cuba since 1862.
Bacardi is available in a 750ml bottle. Price Rs. 300/-

| Concept 6 |

Introducing *Bacardi* rum

"Just Add Bacardi"

When the world weighs heavy on you and you feel like breaking loose ... Just take a slow lazy sip of *Bacardi* on ice and find yourself transported to an exotic land where everything is passionately alive and exhilarating. Because only the smooth, clear taste of *Bacardi* can give you all the life, colour and fun that you desire.

Born in the Caribbean island of Cuba, *Bacardi* goes remarkably well with anything — *Coke*, tonic, juice or simply on the rocks with a slice of lime. Any which way you drink it, you'll love the rhythm and swing *Bacardi* adds to your life.

To spice up your life - just add Bacardi.
Founded in Cuba in 1862.
Bacardi rum is available in a 750ml bottle. Price Rs. 300/-

Usage and attitude study — key findings

A. Penetration & Profiling

* One out of five (21%) people have an alcoholic drink regularly (as seen in the past one month). For women it drops down to 4 per cent as compared to 17 per cent men who drink spirits regularly.
* Penetration is relatively lower in the 18–24 age group (13%).

- Drinking of scotch, vodka and white rum was more predominant towards Mumbai, whereas Indian whisky was concentrated more in Delhi.
- While a majority of the drinkers are in the 25-44 age group, vodka and scotch are predominantly consumed among the younger half of the segment.
- Heavy drinkers of rum and Indian whisky generally belong to the lower social class while the majority of scotch, vodka and white rum heavy drinkers belong to the A1 group.

B. Category Penetration: Usage & Frequency
   (Details relating to only white spirits are given below)

Gin Drinkers
- Highest penetration of white spirits among regular drinkers (62% ever triers and 17% past month drinkers).
- Average frequency of consumption lowest among all categories (2.4 times/month).
- One out of three (34%) gin drinkers consume vodka regularly.
- Higher penetration among the young adults (24%) vs. total (17%).

Vodka Drinkers
- Less than half (45%) the drinkers have tried vodka but only 13 had it in the past month.
- Low average frequency of consumption (92.5 times/month).
- High penetration among young adults (29%) vs total (13%).
- Four out of five (38%) vodka drinkers also consume gin.

White Rum
- Very low ever triers (21%) and past month drinkers (2%).

C. Brand Awareness and Consumption
   (Relating to only white spirits)

White Spirits: *Blue Riband Gin* is a dominant white spirit brand (32%) followed by vodkas — *Smirnoff, Karmazov* and *Alcazar*.

Image Associations: Gin/Vodka — Smooth, light-bodied, mixed with lime/orange, associated with summers, afternoon, women, etc.

The Brand

Brand history

In 1862, Don Facundo Bacardi set up a small tin-roofed distillery in Santiago, Cuba. Here he began manufacturing new *Bacardi* rum, using a formula he had hit upon after many years of experimentation.

Rum was, at that time, a fiery drink used by Caribbean seamen to ward off the cold; Don Facundo's new formulation transformed rum into a smoother, lighter, milder drink, called *Bacardi*. Over the next few years, the rum gained popularity all over Cuba, and Don Facundo began expanding his operations. He kept the formula a closely guarded secret as the Bacardi family's success story took hold. The product was entered in international exhibitions, where it was acclaimed alongside such wonders as A.G. Bell's telephone. His sons dreamt of expanding the brand outside Cuba; Cuba was then on the road to independence, and was aided by a considerable US presence. Put together, these factors gave *Bacardi* rum a foothold in the US, the first step towards becoming a huge international brand.

Today *Bacardi* sells in over 170 countries, its popularity the world over has made it the No. 1 international spirits brand in the world.

The Bacardi Bat

Inspite of six generations of the Bacardi family distinguishing itself in business, philanthropy and public service, easily the most recognisable member of the family remains the one with no name. It is the *Bacardi Bat*, the trademark that appears on the label of every product carrying the Bacardi surname.

Legend has it that Don Facundo's wife, Donna Amalia Lucia Victoria suggested making the bat the trademark for the new rum, perhaps because of the colony of fruit bats living in the rafters of the first Bacardi distillery. Donna Amalia, who was cultured in the arts, believed bats represented a blessing of good health, fortune, and family unity. But this suggestion of hers was also hard-headed and pragmatic. Illiteracy was common in the nineteenth century, and for a product to get recognised and sell, it needed a memorable graphic logo — a trademark. The bat mythology helped. That is the power of mnemonic.

Word of Don Facundo's bat spread around the world along with his smooth new rum. The bats, local storytellers attested, brought good fortune and added magical powers to his rum. Today the *Bacardi* bat is a welcome character in more than 170 countries around the world where *Bacardi* rum is sold and enjoyed. Accomplishing everything it was supposed to do for more than a century, the bat has elevated its presence to new heights.

Bacardi in the Indian context

Alcohol had never been comfortably accepted by post-Independence Indian society. Drinking was generally associated with the darker side of life, with deep and unholy secrets. Dingy bars, seedy-looking characters and drunk villains in Hindi movies, in stark contrast with the clean, honest and upright non-drinking hero—this typified society's outward attitude to alcohol drinking. Further, the absence of international players in the spirits category, as well as comfortably entrenched local brands, meant that the consumer had never been exposed to the glitzy and slick side of spirits marketing until the 1990s came along.

The '90s ushered in the winds of change in the entire social and economic fabric of the country, and like everything else, spirits shifted into gradual movement away from the traditional perception. *Bacardi* was positioned to ride on this change. One of the key elements to be built into *Bacardi*'s brand character was, therefore, its image as 'the icon of new age drinking'. Changing attitudes to drinking were already apparent, in that drinking was gradually coming out into the open, and especially in urban areas, gaining acceptance. By associating with, and by accelerating this process of change in a positive manner, the brand immediately gained relevance in the life of the consumer.

Defining core value

Internationally, the brand statement is:

> The world's original, premium smooth rums, created in Santiago de Cuba in 1862, which captures the freedom, colour and passion of the Latin Caribbean spirit.

In India, Bacardi Carta Blanca's core value was defined as *vibrant sensuality*. This represents an unaffected pursuit of enjoyment through one's senses. *Vibrant* because the character of the brand is passionate, energetic and upbeat. *Sensuality*, strictly speaking is the appreciation through tactile senses (feel, hear, taste…). (In literal terms, sensuality is the overall *sensory* experience surrounding *Carta Blanca*).

Vibrant sensuality therefore means "living life true to your senses" in a style that is energetic and colourful (as opposed to languid or passive pleasure). Within the Bacardi portfolio, *Carta Blanca* is the flagship brand. It is the main image driver of the umbrella brand Bacardi; it is also the Indian consumer's introduction to the brand.

Selling Strategy for Bacardi Carta Blanca

Brand / Product

What is the brand / product to be advertised?

> A range of rums, under the *Bacardi* name; historically better known for white rum and associated with the light-hearted Caribbean spirit of fun, frolic and water.

Brand / Position

What is the position the brand currently holds in the consumer's mind — and why?

> An international brand of (exotic) alcohol.

Brand objective

How do we want the brand to be positioned in the consumer's mind?

> As an icon of new age drinking.

Conceptual target

What 'natural' grouping of consumers, bound by a common set of values, singular outlook, attitudes, aspirations, do we wish to reach?

> Post-liberalisation young adults.

Core desire

What is the conceptual target's most deeply held desire, need, want, hope, that the brand best fulfils?

> Unshackle themselves.

Role of the product

What is the functional/symbolic role of the product category in the lives of the consumer?

> Functional : Relaxant
> Social lubricant
> Gives a high
> Symbolic : Let your hair down... have fun.

Reason to believe

What is the most compelling rationale to support the role of the product?

> Less intense in looks, hence eminently adaptable to broader drinking occasions.

Brand essence

What is the enduring spirit which anchors the brand — and how should it speak to the deeply held values of the conceptual target?

> Vibrant sensuality.

Brand Activities

Television activity

Around the world *Bacardi* has a long association with a 'sun-sea-sand' imagery which has successfully maintained its brand salience, especially during launch phases. This imagery was also found to lend itself perfectly to the positioning developed for the Indian market. The sun-sea-sand route was researched, and was found to be very well received by consumers. This came through on the concept testing study, as well as on quantitative research parameters. The concept that was tested was "*Get away to be relaxed in a carefree world*", via a sun-sea-sand execution. (The first concept in the research section above). Quantitative consumer research showed a strong acceptance of this particular concept, the product and its packaging.

Communication for the brand was led by television advertising, which used the international, 'Friends' commercial. The various elements in the theme TV commercial (sun, sea, sand, free spirited interaction between the sexes) were in sync with the new attitudes to drinking, and with *Bacardi* as an 'icon of new age drinking'. The commercial represented taking drinking out into the open, far away from the dark atmosphere of illicit pleasures.

Below the line activity

This was supported by an extensive below-the-line package for the retail channel as well as on-premise outlets (pubs, bars, restaurants, etc.,). The package developed on the sun-sea-sand theme was intended to maintain high salience levels especially during the crucial launch phase.

One critical element of the *Bacardi* persona was the several promotions that were conducted at pubs and discotheques across the metros in India. The pub-going culture, which is still developing, has got a strong impetus due to *Bacardi*'s popularisation of the concept.

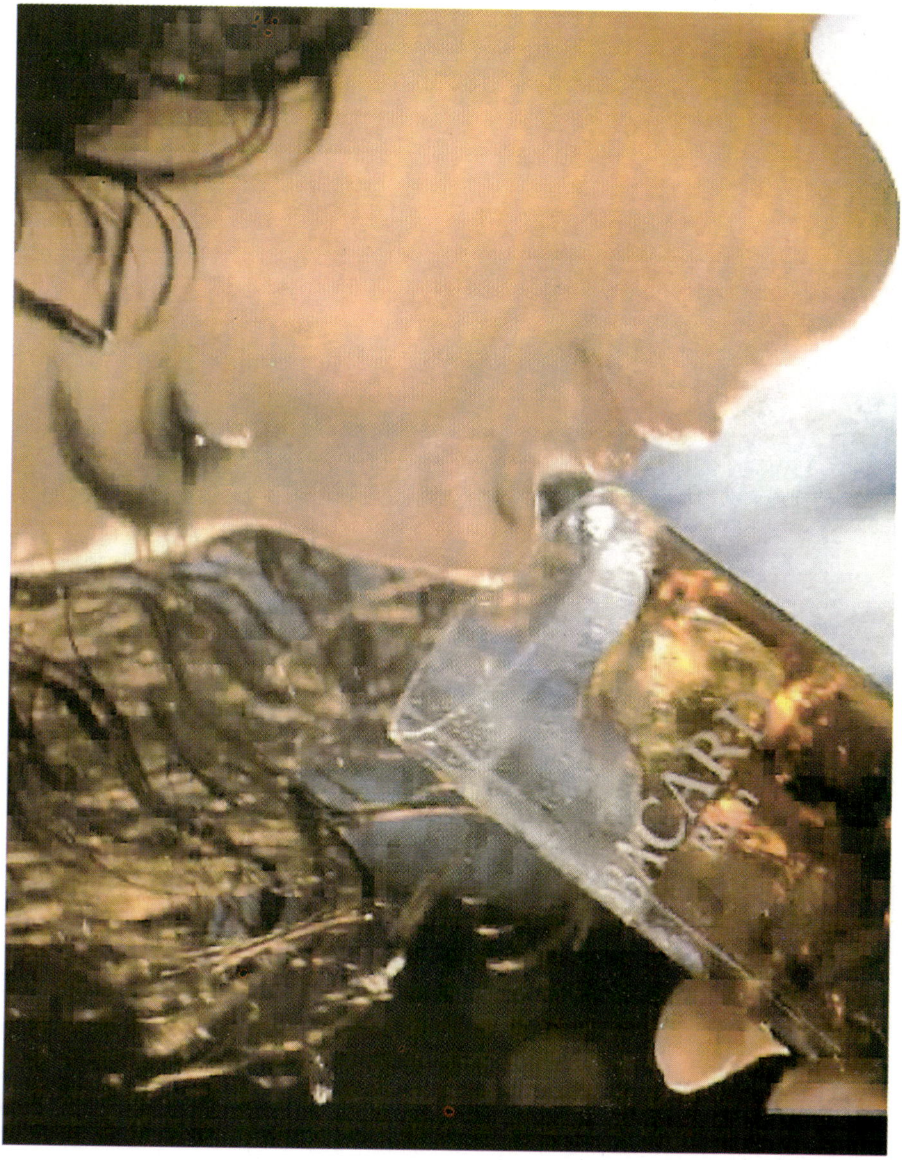

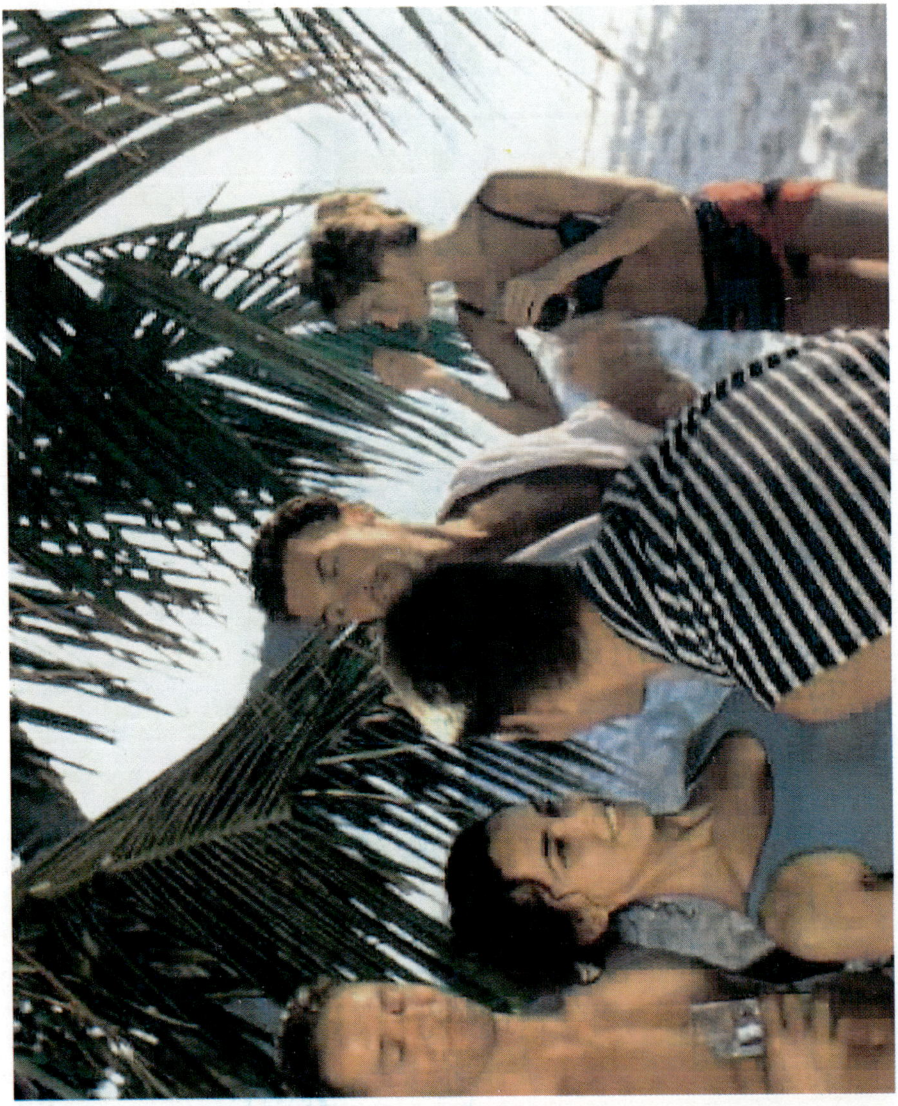

A series of innovative promotion mechanics were designed for these on-premise outlets. The promos served various objectives:
* To announce the launch of the brand, and to give the target consumer a feel of its trendy, young and vibrant character.
* To generate a sampling of the product — this was a critical role given the fact that white rum was still a new product for the consumer.
* To gain substantial incremental volume sales.

Of course the promotions also offered excellent opportunities to develop different elements of the *Bacardi* brand character. They have now been built into the long standing properties of the brand. Some of the key properties are:

"Batstage with Bacardi"

The *Bacardi* core consumer being 18-25 years old and urban, music is an effective medium to use to get through to him. The idea was to sponsor live bands to perform on a given night in pubs and discotheques. This was to be done on a regular basis and branded "Batstage with *Bacardi*". The first such event was a Savage Garden concert in Mumbai in April 1998, followed by one with Diana King. These big events gave the activity momentum that sustained it through the year.

A range of collateral material was designed to create the right ambience for the event. This included posters, tent cards, table mats, coasters, etc. The "Batstage with *Bacardi*" property has ensured that the brand remained topical and very much a part of the young and happening music. It is being used this year as well and is being built up as a long term property of *Bacardi*.

"Latino nights"

The world over, *Bacardi* is seen as having originated in Cuba in 1862, and the heritage built around this idea was an important part of the brand. In India, however, the concept of Cuba means very little, and people's perceptions of it are very hazy. It was therefore decided to concentrate on 'Latin-ness' and not just on Cuba. Latin culture happens to be on an upswing around the world and is seen as energetic, vibrant and rhythmic; fun-loving people like Ricky Martin and Gloria Estefan have further helped popularise this culture. *Bacardi*'s history was therefore to be communicated in this context.

An ongoing event called 'Latino Nights' was created and conducted at pubs and discos in all metros. A Latin ambience was created at the venues using a variety of items from invitations to posters, from Latin music to vinyls. Press ads advertised the event and drew traffic to these outlets. Additionally, special offers and promotional games were used to make the evening an enjoyable one for pub-goers.

"Bacardi Blast"

The *Bacardi* Blast is a property designed to build an association for the brand with partying, and with party music. During the first year, *Bacardi* had tied-up with Channel [V] to popularise the *Bacardi* Blast. The event also attempted to synergistically bring together below the line and above the line activities. A weekly one hour programme with the same name was scheduled on Channel [V]. Below the line, the event was a huge party organised at the most happening discotheque in a city. Every month, the party moved from city to city to cover major nightspots in each. These were then covered on the TV programme, along with the latest hits and dance numbers.

The Blast was a big success below the line in all the cities it went to, and is synonymous with an ultimate party for regular disco-goers. It continued in the second year as well.

Others

Other promotions and activities during the year included: sponsorship of the Asian Beach Volleyball Tournament in Mumbai, sponsorship of a Ricky Martin concert in Mumbai, "Night of the Bat" theme evenings at pubs, and sampling nights at all on-premise outlets.

Marketing Activities

Neck tags: These are hung on every *Bacardi* bottle sold at retail points. They serve to educate the consumer about the different ways

BACARDI
PRESENTS THE

Misbehave tonite.
Repent, Thursdays, 10pm.
Fridays, 10.30pm.

Hot steppers. Hit numbers. Have a blast. But whatever you do, remember Channel V's crew will be there. So, you never know when the camera will be on you. Be there tonite. And be on air on Thursdays and Fridays.

Hosted by Laila and Mark. DJ-Ivan. April 25, Fastrack UFO. 9 p.m. onwards. [V] Coca-Cola

BACARDI 〰 　　　　　　　　　　　　　　　Three Flights Up

IF BRAZIL MAKES YOU CRY, CUBA WILL CHEER YOU UP.

Frankly, we take no responsibility for the way your favourite team will make you feel. You see, it's normal to get excited, or emotional, when watching it all on the king size TV screens put up in here. If your team loses, you can confide in Bacardi - the Cuban delight. Or take part in a contest to win some great prizes. And feel good. Drop in at Three Flights Up before July 13th. We'll do our best to keep you in good cheer.

BACARDI SOCCER MANIA

AN EVENT FULL OF KICKS

of consuming the product, and give him an overall flavour of its colourful and vibrant personality.

On pack promotion: was used during the festival season (Oct-Nov) to provide an additional thrust to short-run volumes. The offer was of two glasses free with every 750ml bottle purchased at retail. The promo was supported with POP that ensured high visibility at point of purchase.

Pitcher promotion: was run at key on-premise outlets in the metros. This activity was held in association with *Coke*; the offer was a discounted price for consumers buying a pitcher of *Bacardi & Coke*. A pitcher contained 5 drinks. On-premise collateral was used to publicise the promotion.

Sampling nights: were organised at all key outlets in all markets. The venue decor was designed so as to create a splash for the brand upon its entry into the city. Sampling was an activity of key importance, given that white spirits in general, and white rum in particular, were new concepts, and the consumer needed an introduction to both the product and the various ways in which it could be consumed. All consumers entering the outlet on a sampling night are given a shot of *Bacardi* with a mixer of their choice (*Coke, Citra*, soda, etc.), in a cup designed specifically for *Bacardi* sampling nights.

Performance

This section covers indicators of the brand's performance in its first year since launch, and a SWOT analysis of *Bacardi* today.

SWOT

Strengths
* Premium international product with world leader credentials
* Successful launch
* Strong advertising (leading to unusually high awareness levels)
* Product acceptability (in terms of taste, mixer versatility, etc.)
* Badge value

Weaknesses
* White spirit imagery is less macho and substantial
* Severe restrictions on advertising limit image-building effectiveness
* Wide mixer appeal dilutes its status as a 'mainline' spirit

Opportunities
* To own the white spirit category
* Drive the trend of on-premise drinking
* Leverage premium and quality status across other categories (e.g., dark rum)
* Develop a *Bacardi* franchise across various consumer segments

Threats
* Government regulations
* Broadcasting bill
* Several new entrants in the international spirits category, and in international beer
* As yet only a single brand offering

The Brand Today

In the first year of launch, *Bacardi* attained and surpassed its volume targets. This can be gauged from the fact that the first year's volumes exceeded those of its closest competitor, *Smirnoff* vodka, a brand that had been established in the market for over 4 years. Initial reports indicate that the volume and its growth are being sustained in the second year of operations. Already, Bacardi Carta Blanca is reported to have garnered over 10 per cent of the international spirits market in India.

In sum, the key to the success of the brand has been not just a quality product, but a complete brand package that meshes in with current social trends and with the needs of today's youth consumers.

4

BRAND RE-POSITIONING

KEO KARPIN HAIR OIL

Background

Until the early '80s, particularly in the Eastern region, the hair oil market was dominated by brands like *Jabakusum, Mahabringaraj* and coconut based oils. These were thick hair oils, which were promoted as ideal for the nourishment and maintenance of strong, beautiful hair. At that time the fashion, particularly for women, was to have long, thick, beautiful hair.

Dey's Medical, a pharmaceutical house in Calcutta, decided to make an entry into this market in 1985, with their hair oil *Keo Karpin*. They found that the thick hair oil market was stagnating with the changing fashion trends which advocated the use of less sticky oil. Besides, all the brands were sold on the generic platform of nourishment and cooling with no clear positioning, and advertising was restricted to only a few stray press ads.

Keo Karpin took advantage of the situation and repositioned itself as the light, non-sticky hair oil that aided styling. It breathed freshness into an increasingly mundane category and, supported by sleek advertising and high visibility (in the newly introduced popular TV medium), carved out a distinctive category for itself — that of light hair oils. As luck would have it, the hair style fashion scenario also changed at about the same time. Women now preferred, what could be called 'fluffy hair', and sometimes short hair, which meant that they needed non-sticky hair oils. As a result, *Keo Karpin* fitted the bill of current hair style requirements with its need for *light* hair oil. Through 1985-88 'me-toos' like *Tata Green* and *Dabur Special* joined the fray but without much success, as *Keo Karpin* exploited a phenomenal growth rate to consolidate its position in the North and the East.

Table 4.1 shows the growth rate.

Table 4.1 *Keo Karpin growth rate (%)*

1985	57.7
1986	23.7
1987	24.2
1988	24.7
1989	18.6

Competitors' Activities

During 1989-90, Marico came out with a two-pronged attack on *Keo Karpin* (*Parachute* and *Hair & Care*). It relaunched *Parachute* as a light and contemporary coconut oil, attempted to refocus users towards a time-tested natural hair oil. Other coconut oil manufacturers followed suit, modernising their own brands and together they started eating into the *Keo Karpin* user base. Launch of *Hair & Care*, a value-added modern option (lightness + nourishment of vitamin E, modern packaging and aggressive advertising) appealed to young consumers.

Keo Karpin was now under pressure to retain its market share. As a result, primary sales stagnated in 1990-91. Further, in 1992-93, primary sales declined. This prompted a total rethinking of the brand.

New Strategy

In 1993-94 therefore, the primary task was to bring the brand onstream once again and to stop erosion. To help understand both the market and the users, qualitative research was undertaken.

MY STYLE IS KEO-KARPIN

Because it's me

My life is a hectic whirl of classes, play rehearsals, doing my bit for the environment, weekend hikes, bright lights and jam sessions...

Keo-Karpin lets me look the way I feel. It nourishes my hair and makes it so soft, so lustrous, so manageable.

I can switch so easily from a casual pony tail to a zany, swinging hair style. Because of Keo-Karpin. And because it's me.

Keo-Karpin
Mildly perfumed, non-sticky hair oil

SO HEALTHY ~ SO BEAUTIFUL ~ SO KEO-KARPIN

Dey's
Dey's Medical
Care you can trust

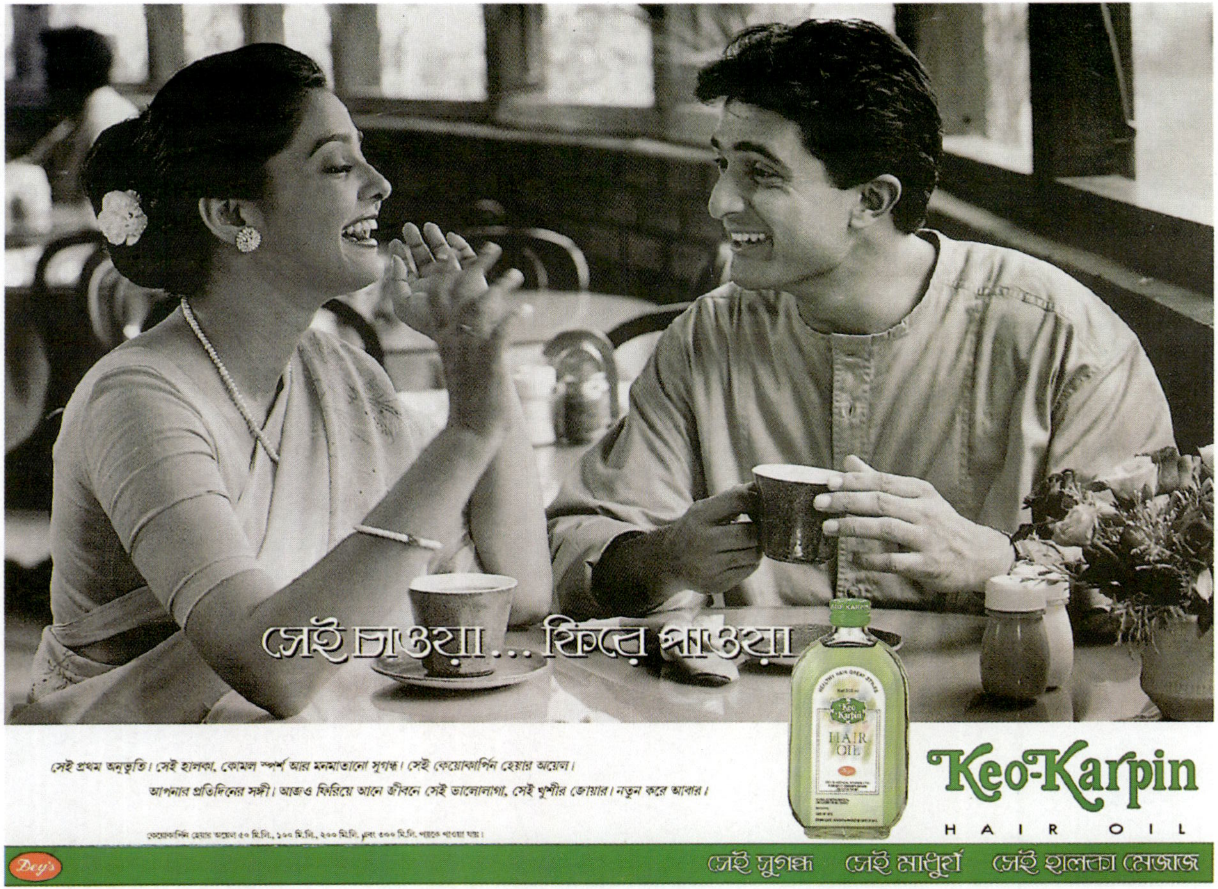

This qualitative research unearthed some valuable insights, such as:

* *Keo Karpin* was, no longer, a modern brand.
* Lightness was not *Keo Karpin*'s exclusive property anymore.
* No physical value addition had been done to the brand *vis-à-vis* the competitive trend of having extra value proposition.
* Yet the brand commanded 67 per cent of the market in the light hair oil category. It was therefore necessary to look at the brand equity balance sheet. This can be summarised as:

BRAND EQUITY LADDERING		KK EQUITY LADDERING
(D) *BONDING*	How do I relate?	(D) KK my intimate confidante
(C) *EMOTIONAL BENEFIT*	What does this mean for you?	(C) Makes me feel young, modern and confident — a new me
(B) *RATIONAL BENEFIT*	What do I do for you?	(B) Gives healthy, manageable hair, I can style it any way I want
(A) *PHYSICAL ATTRIBUTE*	What am I?	(A) Light, nourishing, non-sticky perfumed hair oil

The brand appeal has therefore gone beyond physical attributes. It has created an emotional bond with consumers:

Keo Karpin is a part of me

Communication therefore needed to highlight this bond. Since hair styles were inextricably linked with the brand, they needed to be focussed upon once again.

Creative Execution

To illustrate how "*Keo Karpin* is a part of me" Creative took three important stages in a woman's life, namely, college, marriage and motherhood.

* Three contact points were chosen (shop, home and beauty parlour).
* And the two were blended together in a contemporary setting giving aspirational vibes and indirectly giving support to

nourishment (attractive hair, hair styles and specialist recommendation). This led to the "Mera Hardin *Keo Karpin*" campaign.

Communication worked and the brand started recovering, leading to a growth of 11 per cent in primary sales during 1995-96. Emotional appeal still remained the strongest hook in brand communication — only the context had changed.

During 1996-97 it focussed on mother's care — "*Keo Karpin* ek mamta bhari dekhbhal" — thus successfully countering the high profile campaigning of the competition using the theme of nourishment. During 1997-98 it focussed on the theme, 'yearning for romance', associating it with the contemporary housewives' desire for their husbands' attention. Thus, even in a strong competitive market *Keo Karpin* managed to hold on to its core consumers and registered a growth trend. Table 4.2 gives the latest position.

Table 4.2 *KKHO PRIMARY SALES (KL)*

1997-98	3700 (KL)
1998-99	3900 (KL)
1999-2000 (Est.)	4250 (KL)

Brand Extensions

Taking advantage of the brand equity of the *Keo Karpin* brand, the company decided to extend its activities into allied categories, such as:
(a) Hair problem solver category, with *Keo Karpin* Hair Vitalizer;
(b) Skincare, through launch of body oil leveraging the non-sticky property of the oil (the inherent USP of the *Keo Karpin* brand).

Problem solver

Keo Karpin Hair Vitalizer

Background

Product formulation: 5 internationally accepted proteins and vitamins, Keratin, Biotin, Panthenol, Resorchinol and Nicotinic Acid in alcohol base.

Brand performance

* Sold as a medicinal hair tonic under medical prescription
* Launched in 1983 as an OTC product
* Offering solutions to hair fall and dandruff
* Advt. Testimonial in nature
* Brand steadily grew till 1989
* Post-1989 influx of competition: *Anoop / Oasis / Vaseline Hair Tonic / Pantene / Arnica Plus Triofer.*
* Category slumped and sales stagnated

Research indicated that the reasons were:

* Overclaim — leading to over expectation
* Problem solver nature of the category automatically restricts it to a certain extent of volume growth.

Action taken

Keo Karpin utilized communication as the problem solver, which boosted sales but could not hold on to the consumers, except for those who were very concerned with their problem.

This product category has an inherent drawback. If it solves the problem of 'falling hair', the customer stops using it after sometime. If it fails to solve the problem, the user stops using it anyway, it therefore has a credibility problem. All in all, it is a small and shifting market.

Smart Skincare

KEO KARPIN BODY OIL

Background

Keo Karpin Body Oil was launched in 1990 in the Eastern, Northern and Western Indian markets. After initial success the brand sales stagnated, from '93 onwards. After in-depth discussion within the company, as well as with the advertising agency, it was agreed that the main problems affecting the brand were:

(a) Growth not commensurate with the potential of the product.
(b) The product retention is very high among the loyal users but there are very few new recruits.
(c) The image of Body Oil is dominated by the equity of *Keo Karpin* Hair Oil which is an all-India brand leading the light hair oil category.

Communication Objective therefore for *Keo Karpin* Body Oil was:

(a) Rejuvenate the category (oil in relation to skincare)
(b) Create a sustainable competitive advantage.

And the issues in brand building were: positioning the brand; and defining brand values.

Positioning the brand

Targetted at the young, socially active and confident woman to whom *Keo Karpin* Body Oil is a smart and sensible non-sticky, skin nourisher that keeps the skin soft and healthy through its herbal ingredients.

Therefore, Core Brand values are:
(1) Trusted (2) Natural (3) Traditional, yet contemporary.

Consumer insight

(a) Though oils are considered to be nourishing and essential, convenient and modern products for skincare are being adopted.

"I never wanted to use oil on my body... till I discovered the herbal unoily oil"

KEO KARPIN BODY OIL ISN'T STAINING
Keo Karpin Body Oil is genuinely non-sticky. Once applied, it gets right under my skin in seconds, leaving no stubborn stains on my clothes. No sticky mess, no oily feeling.

I NEED KEO KARPIN BODY OIL, NOT MOISTURISERS
Keo Karpin Body Oil helps my skin retain natural body moisture with **lanolin**, a natural moisturiser. What's more, with **olive oil, arjuna, daruharidra, manjistha, neem** and more, only Keo Karpin Body Oil gives my skin all the goodness of nature.

KEO KARPIN BODY OIL: THE 5 MINUTE RITUAL
To keep my skin soft, smooth and supple all I need is just a few minutes everyday. Why don't you try it too?

Available in 100 & 200 ml. packs

KEO KARPIN BODY OIL

Dey's

For glowing supple skin an ayurvedic oil from Dey's

REMEMBER THE REASONS WHY YOU DON'T USE OIL ON YOUR BODY

Now you can forget them.

MY OIL ISN'T MESSY

Keo Karpin Body Oil is genuinely non-sticky. Once applied, it gets right under my skin in seconds. No sticky mess, no oily feeling.

MY OIL ISN'T STAINING

Most oils are staining. Not Keo Karpin Body Oil. It's genuinely non-sticky, and disappears under my skin in no time at all. Leaving no infuriating stains on my clothes.

I NEED OIL, NOT MOISTURISERS

Keo Karpin Body Oil helps my skin retain natural body moisture with lanolin, a natural moisturiser. What's more, with an exhaustive herbal mix of olive oil, arjuna, daruharidra, manjistha, neem and more, only Keo Karpin Body Oil gives my skin all the goodness that nature provides.

MY OIL ISN'T TIME-CONSUMING

5 minutes a day isn't too much to give for gorgeous skin. Keo Karpin Body Oil makes my skin soft, smooth and supple in just a few minutes. Why don't you try it too?

Dey's KEOKARPIN BODY OIL
The herbal unoily oil that nourishes your skin naturally

Creative task

(a) Bring *Keo Karpin* Body Oil out of the traditional realm by changing the perception that oils are sticky / messy.

Creative strategy

(a) Make the consumer believe that with *Keo Karpin* Body Oil she's getting time-tested and trusted herbal nourishment for her skin.
(b) The consumer should feel convinced that this was the intelligent way to make herself look young and attractive.

Creative magnifier

* The unoily oil

A single press ad in colour was developed which explained, in a very intimate one-to-one manner, how *Keo Karpin* Body Oil had successfully bottled all the benefits of oil, minus its negative qualities. This ad was released in major English and vernacular dailies and women's magazines between October to December '96.

Result

The result surpassed all expectations. The company had initially taken a stiff target for 96-97 (30% increase in sales) for a brand whose sales had remained stagnant for the past 3 years. Within two months of the release the brand sale surpassed its target and forced management to set a fresh target for 96-97, i.e., 500,000 bottles. The company expected to meet its target of 900,000 bottles in 1999-2000.

The company believes that this product has tremendous potential. Although the product is pitched at women, there is nothing stopping men from also using it. Unfortunately there is no data on the total market, and therefore its market share as well, although it is evident that *Keo Karpin* Body Oil dominates the market. However, this brand's sale is expected to exceed 2 million bottles in 3 to 4 years time — double its present sale! Another striking example, where brand extension has proved the power of brand equity!

5

CREATING BRANDS

From Commodity to Branding

Introduction

Commodities stay indistinguishable as long as they are just commodities. As soon as you give the product of a particular company, a name, you have started the brand-building process — an opportunity to differentiate that particular product from several other similar commodities. Differentiation lies at the heart of the theme of branding. Thus differentiation must provide a tangible, unique source of value that can be communicated easily. For, while claiming such differentiation, the brand must create an image, an image of distinguishable benefits. And herein lies the value of a mnemonic — a mnemonic which can visually translate the core value of the product.

This is where advertising plays a crucial role. Once a company has built in such differentiated benefits, particularly with the help of a mnemonic, it becomes so much easier to communicate such tangible benefits to its potential customers. In this manner a brand identity is created. But creating such a brand personality takes its own time and effort and of course money — lots and lots of money. Is it worth the trouble? The answer is YES, an emphatic YES.

Value Focus Approach

In one of the presentations for such a company, advocating branding of their product, Trikaya-Grey Advertising Agency approached the

Creating Brands

problem in a systematic way which can best be illustrated by a graphic. They called it "The Value Focus Approach", of which I have talked earlier. Here I want to talk about two other graphics which are relevant to understand the advantages of the value (read brand) approach [see Figures 5.1 and 5.2].

The first of these two graphics, (Figure 5.1), shows what happens when the product is promoted as a commodity. The second one, (Figure 5.2), on the other hand, shows how the creation of a brand will benefit and sustain profitability and growth. But to achieve that there has to be investment in money and effort over a period.

The next two case studies are examples of how two companies were able to successfully promote their respective products, i.e., turn a commodity into a brand.

THE PITFALLS OF A COMMODITY-LIKE BUSINESS

Vision of customers' needs	Competitors' target and offering	Key comp. lever	Customer loyalty	Competitive intensity	Investment, scope and focus
Similar, generic	All customers, same offering	Lowering price	Low, decreasing	Head to head	Generic; cost, capacity

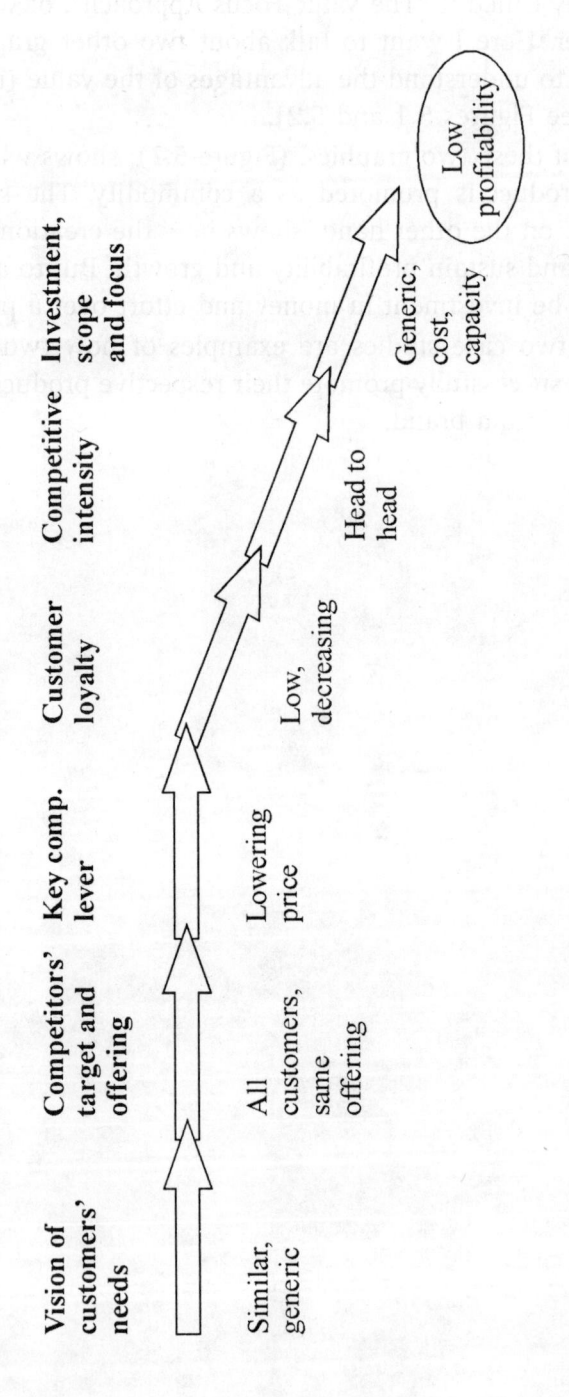

Low profitability

TRIKAYA-GREY

Figure 5.1

THE ADVANTAGE OF THE *VALUE* APPROACH

					Sustained profitability and growth
Different, segmented and quantified	Selected customers, adapted offerings	Creating value by increasing benefits in win-win solutions	Increasing, partnerships reinforced	Differen-tiated	Targeted; service, quality
Vision of customers' needs	Competitors' target and offering	Key comp. lever	Customer loyalty	Competitive intensity	Investment, scope and focus

TRIKAYA-GREY

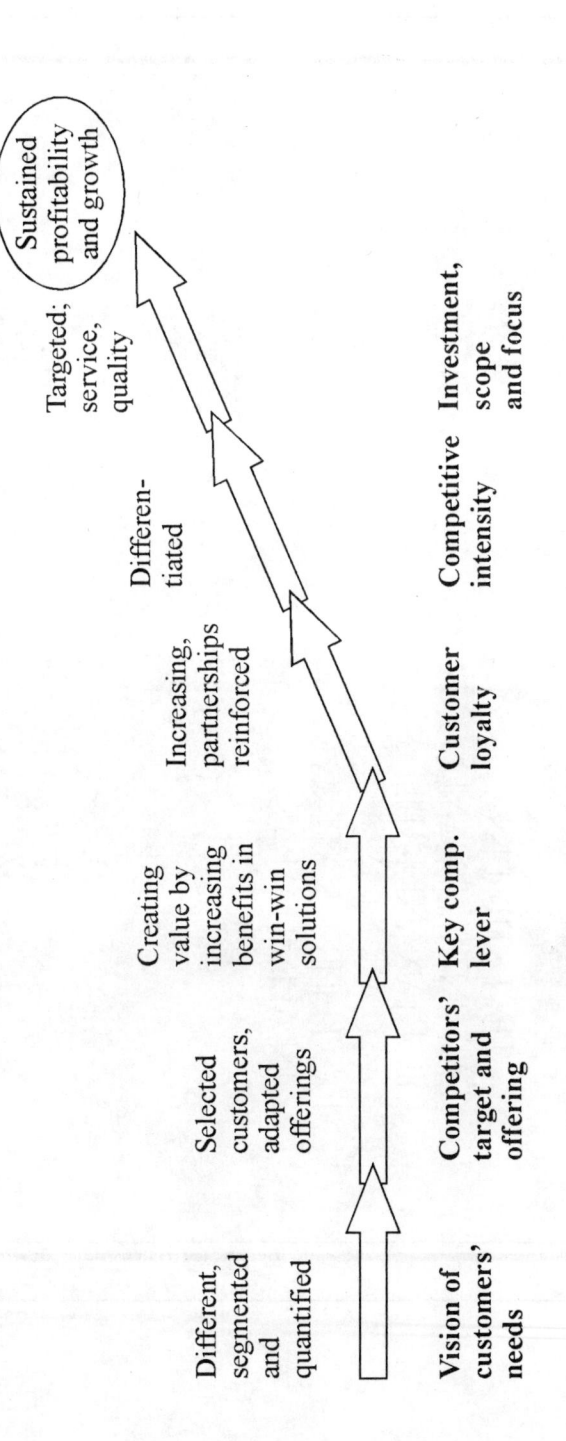

Figure 5.2

LEVI STRAUSS, CALVIN KLEIN AND GLORIA VANDERBILT CAN NOW DO THEIR SHOPPING IN AHMEDABAD.

ARVIND INTRODUCES ORIGINAL DENIM. INDIA'S FIRST. THE WORLD'S BEST.

All these years, the only way to get genuine denim, was to import it.

So you'll be delighted to know it's now freely available in India.

Made by Arvind at India's first denim plant. It's the quality of denim used by the world's best names in jeans.

In fact, it's probably a lot better than the denim you're importing now.

Dimensionally stable. Pre-shrunk. With anti-skewing properties.

In a fabulous range of textures and patterns.

Write in to the Arvind Mills for more details.

And winter too. Before Levi, Klein and Vanderbilt decide to go shopping.

Original Arvind Denim

The Arvind Mills Limited, Naroda Road, Ahmedabad 380 025.

Start of a Brand

ARVIND'S ORIGINAL DENIM

Background

Sometime in the middle of the 1980s Arvind Mills decided to launch denim in India. This was the first time any mill in India was introducing this material and, hence Arvind Mills was very keen to make it a success.

When the matter was discussed with the advertising agency, Trikaya-Grey, the concensus was that the company should introduce the product as a brand. Arvind Mills, even then was a well-known textile mill, and had very good distribution channels to sell its products throughout India. The Arvind name was synonymous with quality fabrics, particularly in certain specialised items like voiles, dhotis, sarees — superior quality, 100% cotton. Another question that was raised in that meeting: why can't denim be sold as quality 100% cotton fabric, also through the same trusted distribution channels.

Market

A study of denim users however revealed that the product was primarily used by the manufacturers of denim trousers and shirts. Relatively, a very small quantity of the material would be purchased directly by the consumers, unlike voiles, dhotis and sarees, or even shirtings. Naturally, therefore, it would make sense to create a separate distribution channel to sell *Arvind's Denim* to these manufacturers directly, thus saving, in the bargain, the middleman's commission. That money could then be ploughed back into advertising and promotion of the product.

The market should as such be big — both immediately, as well as in the future. It was generally known that smuggled denim trousers of well-known brands, like *Levis, Wrangler*, etc., were already available in the market; some of the Indian brands, like *Wings, FU*, etc., were importing, or buying imported denim fabric from the grey market.

It was noted that in a hot country like India, trousers made of 100% cotton fabric should be welcome. Also denim trousers can be worn again and again; and needs less washing comparatively. All in all, therefore, once the trend catches on, the denim market should be enormous. And of course, the size of the population, particularly the middle class, would ensure a huge market. Economic development and industrialisation would also imply a more than average growth in the middle class. It generally appeared that there would be a huge market for a product like denim.

Strategy

Since there was every likelihood that other mills would also start manufacturing denim in the future, particularly if *Arvind Denim* met with success, it was felt that Arvind's denim must have a special identity, so that in the future it could be differentiated from other denims. And what better way to do that than by making it a brand. Thus the concept of introducing Arvind's denim as a brand was conceived.

Accordingly, at the briefing session, Arvind's marketing team and Trikaya's creative team agreed that Arvind's denim would be introduced in the Indian market as a brand. Arvind also informed the agency that quality-wise it would be comparable to the best available anywhere in the world. In fact it would definitely be second to none. Arvind also informed the agency that it was in touch with foreign brands like *Levis, Lee, Wrangler, Gloria Vanderbilt*, etc., to sell *Arvind Denim* to these companies. It therefore meant that the product should be promoted not only as a quality product, but as a product that could match the best, anywhere in the developed world. This fact needed to be factored into the final branding.

Target customers

(1) Primarily, manufacturers of denim trousers and shirts.
(2) Secondarily, users (or consumers) of those trousers and shirts.

Creative objective

As stated earlier, the creative briefing stressed two points:

(1) The product would be promoted as a Brand.
(2) The quality aspects had to be stressed — should be comparable with the best available anywhere in the world.

Agency's recommendation

Accordingly Trikaya presented a series of layouts, which while emphasising the point that the 'product is of world quality', also must stress that it was really as good as the 'original' denim, available in the developed world. That is how the brand was named *Arvind's Original Denim*. In all advertising material, including press, TV, point-of-sale material, hoardings, etc., these words "Original Denim" in a circular, logo form became part and parcel of the advertising campaign. The essence of the brand value was the core proposition of the brand. It was this unique essence that would set apart this brand from the products made by other denim manufacturers in the future.

Distribution

Since it was evident that distribution would play a very important part in the overall marketing plan, it was agreed that a dual distribution system was called for.

(1) For manufacturers of trousers and shirts — direct selling by the company's representatives, thus eliminating all middlemen. This would also help in getting quick feedback about the quality from these manufacturers.
(2) For consumers, and those small manufacturers who preferred to buy from dealers (mainly because of credit facilities) appointment of Preferred Dealers or Wholesalers. Care was taken to have a limited number of such dealers, so that they would take interest, particularly in the initial stages, to store and sell the product. After all, this was a new product for them.

Execution of the Advertising Campaign

Once the advertising campaign was finalised, it was released throughout India, both in the electronic media, i.e., TV, and in the press. To give the campaign the 'Original flavour', well-known American icons were superimposed, as will be evident from the reproduction of one of these ads here.

It is to be noted here that the advertising agency, as well as the company, treated the product as if it was a fast-moving consumer product; and gave the necessary inputs to make sure that the campaign was visible to all the potential consumers of the finished products manufactured out of the 'Original' denim. Obviously, the buyers of the denim fabric, who then converted the fabric into trousers and shirts, were also automatically exposed to these media inputs.

Performance

Inspite of some initial hiccups, *Arvind's Original Denim* is a success story. Not only did the product do well in the Indian market, the company was able to sell the material to almost all the leading manufacturers of branded denim products such as *Levis, Wrangler, Lee,* etc., in the developed market. In fact, export became such an important market, that Arvind had to open offices in New York, London and Hong Kong. Eventually it became the third largest manufacturer of denim in the world. The fact that other well-known textile mills followed Arvind into this new field, in the years to follow, tells its own story. Today when you talk of denim, you automatically think of *Arvind's Original Denim!*

WE HARVEST 40 MILLION METRES OF DENIM.

MUST BE THE ATTENTION WE PAY TO THE SOIL, SEEDS AND FERTILIZERS.

The finest cotton in India grows on the fertile plains of Punjab.

So, we at Arvind located a permanent office there.

Our experts constantly monitor planting, picking, staple length and fibre thickness in select fields.

Only the best raw cotton is then sent to our denim plant in Ahmedabad.

A place where elaborate on-line checks scrutinise every millimetre of yarn produced.

This relentless pursuit of quality even drove us to spend one year with technical experts from Tsudokoma, Japan.

To pioneer an air-jet loom to weave fine 14.5 oz denim, which produces larger volumes at greater consistency.

Our Sucker Muller equipment ensures constant dyeing depth, while our foam-finishing process adds the final touches.

The fruits of such labour have been sweet.

Growing by leaps, bounds and repeat orders.

A third of the 40 million metres of denim that we produce is sent to developed nations like the US, UK, Canada and other West European countries.

Repeat orders alone accounted for 80% of these exports.

A rather fitting testimony to the timeliness of our delivery schedules.

Our Uster 10 rating, moreover, catapults us to the front rank of denim manufacturers worldwide.

All of which only inspires our in-house R&D department to continually find ways to enhance denim quality.

While our offices in New York, London and Hong Kong ensure that service is round-the-clock and round-the-corner.

Which merely goes to confirm the old adage:

As you sow, so shall you reap.

Arvind
DENIM

Arvind Worldwide (USA) Inc. 150 West, 42nd Street, Suite 614, New York 10036, U.S.A. Contact: Mr. Kirit Vaidya. Phone No:(212) 768 4815 Fax No: (212) 768 7578. Arvind Worldwide (M) Inc. 802, Park Tower, 15, Austin Road, Kowloon, Hong Kong. Contact: Mr. Y.V.L. Pandit. Phone No : (852) 735 0229. Fax No: (852) 375 3875. Arvind Worldwide (M) Ltd. 120 Wilton Road, Vigilant House, Victoria, London, SW1V1JZ. Phone No: (071) 828 9817. Fax No: (071) 828 6297. The Arvind Mills Ltd., Naroda Road, Railwaypura Post, Ahmedabad 380 025, India. Contact: Mr. S. Padmanabhan. Phone No: (91-272) 312459/377002 Fax No: (91-272) 378267/371396.

Giant Strength
Ambuja Cement

How a Company Converts a Commodity into a Brand

GUJARAT AMBUJA CEMENT

This is precisely the story of *Gujarat Ambuja Cement*. Back in the mid-1980s when the Managing Director of the company approached Trikaya-Grey for a session as to how the then new company's product, i.e., cement, could be promoted through advertising, the meeting ended with an open question: could Gujarat Ambuja's cement be converted into a brand. If it could be, then only would the customers ask specifically for the brand, and not just for a bag of cement. Naturally the product needed to be promoted as a brand, and not as a commodity.

It was a bold move, since the general usage pattern of cement did not lend itself to being seen as a brand. On the other hand, if it could be given the status of a brand, it would not only be able to give itself an identity, but what was probably more important, the Advertising Agency and the Marketing Team could then create and build a brand, and thus give it a unique status amongst the various bags of cement available in the market at that time.

Both the company and the advertising agency accepted the challenge. Over the next few years they were able to successfully launch the product as a brand. And thus history was created.

This is the story of that singular creation.

The Market

A study of the market revealed that the market was governed by commodity trading. Those who interface with cement can be divided into:

(1) Those who produce cement, such as a company like Gujarat Ambuja.
(2) Those who use cement, i.e., the construction industry.

However, the construction industry has multiple segments:
* The Dealer or Dealers through whom cement is sold.
* The Builder, who buys that cement. This includes home builders as well.
* The Mason/Contractor who actually uses the cement.

The target audience therefore can be divided into two main categories:

(1) The Trade, i.e., dealer or dealers who actively deal in this category. (It was also noticed that the market was strongly distribution led. For obvious reasons it was largely a 'commodity' market [and still is], where all cements were seen as similar. Naturally price became a very important element. Obviously the dealers' recommendation played a very important role.)

(2) Actual users (masons/contractors) also played a part in the recommendation of a choice. But until then no company had talked directly to this segment, other than the dealer from whom the cement was being bought.

There is, of course, another segment of the target audience, namely, 'the individual homeowner'. One can even call 'this segment' the secondary target audience. However, he belongs to a category that only finances the purchase. His involvement with cement is generally low, for he is more interested in the finished product, i.e., the home for which he is paying. He therefore, depends on the trade for 'expert' advice. To be fair, brands like *Haathi, Lotus, ACC,* and *Narmada* did exist, and company name and equity were also used to differentiate and recommend, but only on a lower scale.

The Strategy

When the Creative Team of Trikaya and the Marketing Team of Gujarat Ambuja Cement met to work out their 'strategy', they took into account the following:

The objective

Since they were a cement company, and had no corporate equity to use as leverage, there was a need to consciously identify a difference in the product so as to make it special. The task therefore was to create a brand called 'Ambuja'.

To achieve the above objective it was agreed that a route be adopted which would cut through the walls between segments of the market, and directly address the needs of the individual house-owners, as well as the actual users, the mason and the contractor. However, it was agreed that if the brand was going to project the product as the best in the market, the brand must offer superior quality, that is, superlative strength. Research also revealed that 'strength' was the one overwhelming benefit desired from cement by all sections of the audience. Furthermore:

* It must be of consistent quality.
* It must generate reliable supplies.
* It must demonstrate superiority. This is where the use of a suitable mnemonic became a necessity, later creatively rendered as 'the Giant Strength of *Ambuja Cement*'.

Redefined target

The dealer remained the major player in the brand push. Masons became an important additional set of recommendees. Technical services were created to reach the network via the services team.

Training programmes for the masons were started for the first time. The result was spectacular. Not only were the skills of these people enhanced, there was evidence of emotional indebtedness to the company as well. As a result the company became an ally and not just a supplier. This emotional bonding with the network played an important part in the transformation of a product into a brand.

Pricing

It was agreed that there should be uniformity of price, for which was required strict price control. It was realised that along with the control on price, there had to be control on the credit terms so that there was fairness across the entire segment. This in turn, would ensure a fair margin for the dealer. Thus there was no need to resort to price-cutting through discounts, etc. This in turn would ensure good stock flow planning.

Relationship building

To consciously create a sense of belonging, "The Ambuja Parivar" was created. Activities included dealer conferences/meetings, awarding of shares, family gatherings, celebration of festive occasions/personal milestones, scholarships for children's education, etc., so as to make everybody feel that they were part owners of the brand, and not just recipients of gifts and prizes.

Talking to the consumer

The customer knows very little about cement. He does not understand or recognise the differences that exist between one brand and another. So he relies heavily on the recommendations made by those he considers his expert panel, i.e., the actual users, namely masons.

By providing information to the consumer, i.e., the individual houseowner, his involvement will become higher in the first purchase, as he is then involved in the economies of the purchase, and in creating his channels of credit. Since his only understanding of cement is that it should have strength, the need for a suitable mnemonic became a very important element in the communication objective. Also as far as individual houseowners are concerned, because of the high indifference/ignorance of this category, the company saw a unique opportunity for creating a brand image. By moving these people from a state of indifference to one of familiarity, the company would be able to make them ask the trade specifically for the *Ambuja* brand.

Creative objective

Trikaya-Grey realised that there were some limitations to this communication. Cement was, by its very nature, a low involvement category. They also realised that the basic reassurance sought was of strength, which in a way was intrinsic to the category itself. They also realised that they needed to set it apart from the rest of the category by using unique images, especially those denoting superlative strength. Their brand of cement would therefore provide the benchmark for all other cements, especially through the mnemonic for superlative strength. This focus on super strength would invariably set the product a few notches above the rest of the competition, thereby truly demonstrating product performance.

Thus the clear task of the creative team was to create/use a simple tool for immediate identification of the brand with its message of tremendous strength. The creative platform developed for this product was: 'The Giant Compressive Strength of *Ambuja Cement*'. Considering the low interest levels generated by this category the company had to coax the buyer's interest by reassuring him about the great strength of this product, in the easiest possible manner. Thus the need for the creation of an icon for *Ambuja Cement* — a giant figure of immense musculature, holding massive concrete structures with great ease.

The solution

To create a comparatively simple visual depicting a formidable giant symbolising comprehensive strength, which by itself would become the main message. This would give the individual houseowner a face to relate to, so that instead of remaining only a visual to attract attention, the mnemonic would stand for all that we want him to feel about building his dream home with *Ambuja*. The visual mnemonic creates a medium for immediate identification, i.e., brand identification.

Such a mnemonic should be adaptable across all media, such as press, TV, hoardings, etc. Also it should be extendable to the point of purchase materials. It also gave an opportunity for the educated mason to identify the brand with the visual mnemonic. The mnemonic itself being the message, it has the deliberate advantage of communicating the message without diluting comprehension. The mnemonic also has the advantage of longevity. Indeed the giant strength of *Ambuja Cement* is as relevant today as it was 10 years ago!

Result

The company were the first to convert the IOH segment from a financier to play a more active role in the decision-making activity of choosing the right brand of cement, as there was an image he could relate to which enabled him to identify the brand from the rest, thus moving the category from being a commodity to a brand. The result was all-pervasive. The brand reached the ultimate position of being the pioneer/leader among cements. Demand push from the IOH enabled the company to command a premium — the ultimate test for a brand.

Additionally, an offer of technical services to the mason, as well as having an expert on hand as a supervisor, improved credibility, thus strengthening the leadership imagery. No wonder *Gujarat Ambuja Cement* became the leader within its area of operation. Its market share even today in the area where it first started operating, i.e., Gujarat and Mumbai, is apparently 30 and 50 per cent respectively.

Diamonds as a Brand

DE BEERS

Background

De Beers Consolidated Mines Ltd., manages the consumer demand for gem diamonds and diamond jewellery in 34 countries through advertising, publicity and trade programmes.

In 1992, with the winds of liberalisation blowing, De Beers decided to add India to the list of countries where it runs active marketing programmes.

1993: Setting the Scene & Market Potential

India has a well-established reputation for being the world's largest market for gold. The privately held gold in the country is estimated at over 200 billion dollars (about 4 times the amount held in Fort Knox and about a fifth of all the gold ever mined in the world). The amount would pay the national debt 6 times over. 85-90 per cent of the gold that comes into India is used in jewellery — our national obsession.

India is also the largest buyer of new gold, mined like diamonds, in countries across several continents. In 1993, India consumed approximately 400 tonnes of gold — mostly legal since the repeal of the Gold Control Act in 1992. In retail value, this would amount to around 7 billion dollars or a whopping Rs. 21000 crores (at 1993 exchange rates of Rs. 30/- to the USD). Compared to the gold context, the share of diamonds is miniscule. In 1993, total retail sales of diamond studded jewellery were $415 million dollars [Rs. 1275 crores only(!)]. Since this included the value of gold and other precious stones also used in the jewellery, diamonds alone contributed an even lower figure than that, i.e., a share in the total jewellery market of around 6 per cent.

1993/4/5: Baseline Measurement

Three studies form the baseline measurement of the Indian market. They are:

* *The Diamond Acquisition Study – 1992 & 1995:* These two studies quantitatively measured the market and provided cues for strategy and programme development. They measured occasions of acquisition, what was acquired, in what price range, the purchase process (who bought the piece, how, etc.), and also measured consumer attitudes towards gold, diamonds and other precious stones.
* *The Trade Structure Study – 1994:* This was a complete census of all jewellers in the 53 largest cities of India, to determine their turnover, stocking patterns for gold and diamonds and the process of manufacturing and sourcing of the jewellery. For the purposes of comparison with a later study, only the result for the top 10 cities will be shown here.
* *The Brand Tracking Study (BTS) – 1996:* This annual study was first conducted in January, 1996 and subsequently in January, 1997 for comparison. It is purely and simply, a measurement of consumer attitudes and behaviour towards diamond jewellery and also a measurement of recall and effectiveness of advertising.

The highlights of the three studies are given below as relevant for programme and advertising development. The total market was defined as comprising three segments:

(1) The wedding segment as measured by addressing the newly-wed.
(2) The non-bridal segment, i.e., singles and post-marital acquisition.
(3) The elite segment — the few super rich who acquire high value pieces on a regular basis.

The wedding segment

* In 81 per cent of the cases, parents and relatives of the bride and groom had arranged the marriage and therefore bought the

jewellery. Only in rare instances did the groom and the bride decide for themselves.
* Net acquisition of precious jewellery (excluding silver and costume jewellery) in the ABC socio-economic classes was 99 per cent.

The post-marital segment

* Unlike in the wedding segment, here the occasions of acquisition were much more varied. They are given below.

Occasions for Acquisition

Wedding Anniversary	12%
Birth of Child	5%
Birthday	5%
Diwali/Dassera	2%
No Special Occasion	45%

* The balance is a kind of wedding acquisition. The hypothesis is that much of the 'No Special Occasion' buying is actually advance buying for a daughter's eventual wedding, as and when cash happens to be available.

Consumer attitudes

* Attitudes are measured in two ways — first, as a stand alone agree/disagree score for diamond jewellery on a number of statements and second, as a comparative association with other forms of jewellery. As can be expected, the main competition comes from gold.
* As is apparent from Table 5.1, the attitudes that are positive have to do with a diamond's beauty, and its eternal appeal (forever).
* The attitudes that are negative are economic and knowledge based. Most consumers believe diamonds are too expensive to buy, cannot tell the difference between real and fakes, and are uneasy about buying since they do not know enough.

Table 5.1 DJ Attitudes

	% Agreeing a lot/somewhat	% Disagree
Symbol of love between man and woman	35	42
Suitable for a family heirloom	51	35
Good way to invest money	40	45
Impossible to tell difference between real and fake	70	20
Appeal is forever	64	22
Symbol of success	46	38
Worth the expense	60	29
One larger diamond is more wonderful than DJ with many small diamonds	52	31
Too expensive to buy	89	7
More beautiful than other precious stones	80	12
I am uneasy about buying as I do not know much about them	80	14
I think diamonds are liked because they are expensive	47	42

* Extensive qualitative research into attitudes towards diamond jewellery versus gold threw up the following differences and similarities between the two.

Competitive Positions

Gold	*Diamonds*
Traditional	Modern
Common	Special
Old-fashioned	Young
Investment	Eternal
	Ultimate gift of love

* To an extent, this also reflected an attitudinal position — that diamonds be seen as more modern and aspirational as compared to gold, which would then become reinforced as traditional and commonplace.

Trade Structure Study, 1994

* Only three parameters were set up here — the total number of diamond jewellery outlets, the percentage of diamond outlets to total outlets and the distribution by classification of the various diamond outlets.

Table 5.2 *Jewellery & Diamond Jewellery Outlets: 1994*

City	Jewellery Outlets	Diamond Outlets	% Diamond Total Jewellery
Mumbai	1884	398	21
Delhi	1267	362	29
Calcutta	1872	198	11
Chennai	517	202	39
Bangalore	445	157	35
Jaipur	666	59	9
Ahmedabad	660	64	10
Hyderabad	213	67	34
Coimbatore	579	88	15
Pune	322	61	19

Table 5.3 *Distribution of Diamond Outlets (By Class): 1994*

	Outlets
Class I	155
Class II	194
Class III	541
Class IV	766
Unclassified	—
Total	1656

Marketing Strategy: Early 1995

With all the research outlined earlier, the elements of the marketing strategy were clear:

* Persuade consumers to include diamonds in their gold jewellery purchases as an add-on, rather than as a direct substitution.
* Persuade the trade to increase stocking and display of diamond jewellery, in addition to the gold jewellery they were already showing.

The key opportunities where diamonds could be promoted were clearly two:

(1) The wedding opportunity, could be seen as an extended acquisition occasion, which starts from the moment a daughter is born. This was clearly the single largest occasion for acquisition, but was a one-time shot which did not aim to create an ongoing, repeat purchase customer relationship with diamonds. Also, the number of women getting married in any one year was much smaller than the total number of women in the target audience with the capability and desire for diamond jewellery. To an extent, seeing the wedding as the culmination of many years of acquisition, addressed the issue of continuous buying. Here the acquisition was clearly a gift from the parents to their daughter.

(2) The post-marital acquisition, which could be seen as a huge opportunity in terms of the number of women in the target audience. Even though that also was an opportunity, the acquisition rates were clearly lower. There were two options here: to look at the woman as a self purchaser buying for herself with the husband's approval, but without his involvement; or to look at the husband as the romantic surprising his wife.

Women in research preferred the latter option, even though they said that the final purchase would probably be undertaken by women themselves. Again, strangely enough, it seemed that, a sense of status could be obtained by telling everybody that it was a gift of love even if the item was bought by themselves.

Choosing the Positioning for Diamonds

* The relevance of the 'international symbol of love' positioning was debated given the lack of opportunity/tradition/custom/social acceptance for the groom to buy his bride a diamond. The key motivation for purchase of diamond jewellery for weddings was unquestionably status and 'respect' for the parents of the bride. However, concept statements that selected this, no matter how toned down the implications of status, were rejected outright. It seemed that the moment diamonds were purchased, the status was automatic and consumers did not want to be reminded of crass reasons for the actual purchase.
* On testing the 'symbol of love' positioning, it emerged that it was a highly emotion charged surrogate for status. Consumers found it highly motivating and they seized on it as a socially acceptable way of showing status. 'Symbol of love' also reflected every consumer's inherent desire to be seen as doing the modern thing, rather than being stuck in the traditional mould.
* For these reasons, the 'symbol of love' positioning was selected as most appropriate and motivating for diamond jewellery.

The cascading effect could be visualised thus:

Marketing Strategy: 1995

Create desire for diamond jewellery

↓	↓
Parents-daughter	Post-marital acquisition
↓	↓
Symbol of parental love	Symbol of romantic love
↓	↓
Modernity	*Modernity*
The girl herself as a working woman, confident and capable.	The couple, their relationship. The specialness of the occasion.

On this basis, two commercials were created — Architect, which addressed the parents-daughter opportunity, and Hotel, which addressed the post-marital acquisition opportunity.

1996 Onwards: The Trade Efforts

In conjunction with the advertising efforts, the Diamond Promotion Service (DPS) began a series of trade education and contact programmes. The essential effort was to professionalise the trade, educate it in modern selling methods and to give them the sales aids that would help educate consumers better. Starting April 1996, the DPS covered in extensive seminars, 324 retail outlets in 1996 and 630 in 1997. In 1998, 1008 retailers have attended these education courses, making it a grand total of almost 2000 retailers who have been trained by the DPS. The demand for these courses is generated through word of mouth alone, for a lot of retailers it is a matter of immense prestige to have attended a De Beers programme. It also creates a tremendous market buzz to attend and implement the lessons learned from these programmes.

In addition to the education courses, the DPS also toured the five main cities with a launch conference introducing the advertising and

We don't own bungalows or tea estates or a fleet of cars. Oops... I almost said, "Or diamonds."

Dad, What is it about my diamonds that touches my heart so deeply? It must be the sparkle. Or the rarity. Or the love of those who give it. I feel so proud to be their daughter. It's hard to believe something as magical as diamonds doesn't cost the earth. All of which adds up to make me the proud owner of the most precious thing in the world. Love.

I feel so beautiful in my new diamond earrings. Chosen with care by Mum and

DIAMOND BUYING GUIDE

Check the 4Cs that determine a diamond's quality and value. CUT Unlocks a diamond's natural brilliance COLOUR The closer a diamond is to being colourless, the greater is its value. CLARITY The clearer it is, the more valuable it becomes. CARAT WEIGHT The weight of a diamond is measured in carats. 100 carats make a carat.

	10 POINTS	20 POINTS	30 POINTS
	Rs 2500-5000	Rs 7700-11800	Rs 13500-29000

The price of a diamond varies according to its size and quality. For a diamond of good quality, you should expect to pay:

For more information on diamonds, ask your jeweller or write to De Beers, the world's diamond experts since 1888, at Diamond Information Centre, P.O. Box No. 1867, G.P.O. Mumbai.

DE BEERS
A DIAMOND IS FOREVER

Client: De Beers
Duration: 30 sec

Prod: Hotel Suite

FVO: I shouldn't be doing this.
MVO: I have taken care of things.
FVO: I am a married woman.
MVO: I am a married man.

MVO: You have waited for too long for this.

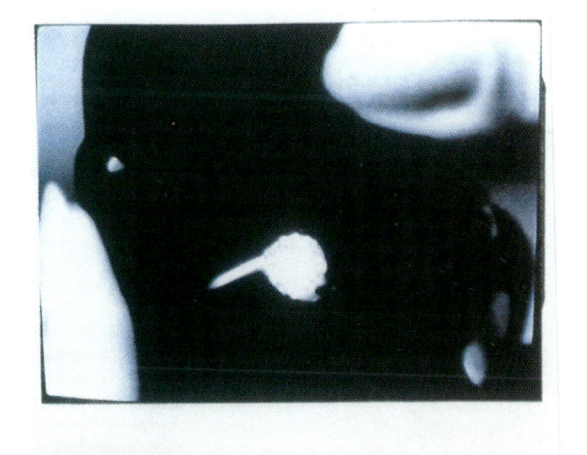

ANC: A diamond born in the earth

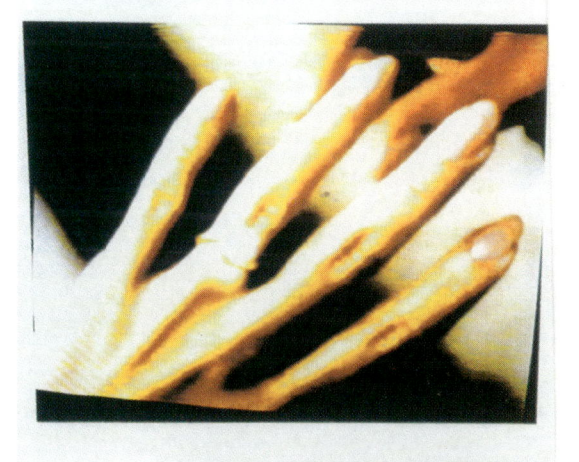

reborn on the

woman you love.

(Phone ring)
MVO: Hello
Kid: Dad, have you given mom the ring?
MVO: Yes son, she loves it.

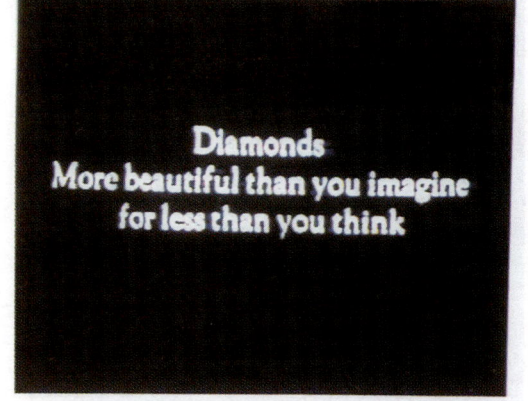

SUPER: Diamonds, more beautiful than you imagine for less than you think.

trade programmes in May 1997. The impact of all of that was seen in August 1997, when the second trade census was done in the top cities. The results of that are shown, with the numbers from the 1994 trade census alongside for easy comparison.

Table 5.4 *Jewellery & Diamond Jewellery Outlets*

City	1994 Diamond Outlets	1997 Diamond Outlets	1997 vs. 1994 % Growth
Mumbai	398	701	76%
Delhi	362	930	157%
Calcutta	198	246	24%
Chennai	202	264	31%
Bangalore	157	322	105%
Jaipur	59	220	273%
Ahmedabad	64	87	36%
Hyderabad	67	138	106%
Coimbatore	88	160	82%
Pune	61	78	28%

This spectacular growth is clearly at the expense of gold jewellery retailers and also marks their evolution into becoming diamond retailers as well. This can be gleaned from the fact that the total number of jewellers went up from 1656 to 3146—a whopping growth of 90%.

Table 5.5 *Distribution of Diamond Outlets (By Class)*

	1994 Outlets	1997 Outlets	% Growth
Class I	155	212	37
Class II	194	358	85
Class III	541	786	45
Class IV	766	1117	46
Unclassified	—	673	—
Total	1656	3146	90

Interestingly, even in Class I, the elite among the jeweller fraternity, conversions to diamond jewellery stocking are happening at a healthy 37%. This is gratifying because most of the really large jewellers would have been expected to deal in both gold and diamond jewellery from the beginning.

Diamonds in the Media: PR Efforts

The third branch of the Diamond Marketing Group — the Diamond Information Centre had been active through 1996 and 1997, creating print and editorial endorsement for diamonds. DIC gets this publicity through photofeatures, fashion shows, interviews, contests, exhibitions and celebrity endorsements. Its role is to provide information, create the impression that diamonds are fashionable and modern, and to supplement the advertising.

In 1996, DIC achieved 125 print placements, 150 minutes of free airtime adding up to a publicity value of Rs. 3.47 crores. And in 1997, the multiplier effect was working harder, because the total investment was only a fifth of that.

1997 in advertising

In 1997, the main campaigns were Parents-Daughter (Architect) and Post-Marital Acquisition (Hotel) on television and the price and knowledge campaign in print (finally!). The major change was in media, where the campaigns were broadcast on Doordarshan for the first time from mid-May onwards.

Table 5.6 *Diamond Sales*

Year	Rs. Crores
1995	2373.2
1996	2625.4
1997	3159.3

Postscript

As De Beers controls 80% of the world's total diamond business, the company realised that if it could increase the use of diamonds (as distinct from gold), the company would automatically reap the benefit of their efforts. They have not therefore promoted the brand De Beers *per se*, but instead the brand 'Diamond' — a clever way to get more business.

6

COMPANY / PRODUCT BRANDING

The Story of Time in India

TITAN

Background

There was a time when owning a watch was a momentous event. It was seen as the first step into maturity, if not adulthood. This was also the time when buying a watch was similar to buying a car — the choice was limited and the product was purely functional. And, like the cars, about two to three decades dated in terms of technology.

The story of the Indian watch industry is perhaps a tale of time standing still, at least for the first four decades after independence. In fact, till 1960-61, the Indian watch industry was totally dependent on duty-free, high quality imports. But these, too, were limited to the most expensive of that period – *Titoni, Rolex, Omega, Sandoz*. Keeping track of time, was perceived to be a luxury meant only for the rich.

The government, however, made the first major effort to produce watches in the organised sector. In 1960, HMT, in collaboration with Citizen, began producing watches in the country. But these remained the mechanical kind, almost till 1981. Even until 1984, only a quarter of the production was that of quartz watches. All along, rampant smuggling of Swiss watches continued, and such was their demand, and supply, that they remained an affordable commodity for the middle class.

It was in this scenario that the Tatas decided to enter the Indian watch industry, with a thorough understanding of the worldwide trends in watches as their starting point. Two factors seemed critical to the success of any watch manufacturer, i.e., cutting edge technology (quartz) and styling (whether elegant, sporty or other). And the Tatas believed that they had the ability to deliver on both.

Even then, this entry was a momentous decision, considering that everybody — consumers as well as dealers — were fairly complacent and satisfied with what was available. HMT had a 90 per cent market share, and few found reason for complaint with the product. Those wanting more could just opt for the imported stuff.

Researching the market ...

The first step for Titan, as with any serious product launch, was consumer research. The first round was conducted in 1986. Given that the market was mostly comprised of mechanical watches, potential buyers of quartz watches were researched. Factors governing purchase decisions, including opinions about the competition — HMT, Citizen and Allwyn — were surveyed. At that time manufacturers' reputations, followed by styling were clearly the factors critical to consumers. Given the Tata backing, it would seem that Titan was on safe ground.

... to relocate your product

By 1987, just before entry, further research into the existing product scenario revealed the following consumer perceptions:

* Mechanical watches were — Durable, reliable, easy to repair, affordable.
* Imported watches were — Emotionally satisfying status symbols, yet 'risky' to buy, as they were not backed by guarantees, and might also be counterfeit.

There seemed to be a clear case of watches being divided into two segments — those that delivered sufficiently on performance, and those that brought great emotional satisfaction.

Titan: Shifting the paradigm

What then could Titan be? Titan sought to enter the market with quartz technology, with the rationale that it was modern, international and cost-effective. To this end a 16-acre ultra modern factory was set up at Hosur at a cost of Rs. 40 crores — one of the world's most advanced and fully integrated manufacturing complexes. All were working towards a launch date within 2 years of the last research, i.e., 19 April 1987.

Given that the technological edge was assured, could Titan then be the high-precision watch? There was obviously no real need for this, and the position already belonged to HMT, the "timekeepers to the Nation".

Given the range of the products, could it then, be the emotionally satisfying status symbol? Again, this was the reserve of the expensive imports.

The process of brand building, Titan knew, would have to start from the very beginning. The product story was, after all, fairly well defined:

> To develop and adopt an integrated marketing approach that ensures that consumers get what they want in terms of design, an international level of quality at an acceptable price, backed by efficient after-sales service.

Titan knew that the only way to be noticed and to be successful was to redefine the product category itself. The Titan product, therefore, was defined not as a watch, but as a personal wear accessory.

The many Ps of the Paradigm Shift

After all possible research, Titan entered the Indian market courageously, with a product that was aimed to enter the national mind-set *as a personal accessory*.

For the first time, there was a product that offered not only reliable timekeeping, but also the emotional satisfaction of wearing a fashionable accessory.

It is worth noting how, for its public face Titan's stress was on the latter, with other elements of the marketing mix being allowed to

TITAN
ROYALE
Ladies dress watch. Created to enhance formal wear. With delicately braided bracelet. 18 ct gold plating. Rs. 1062*
Why risk buying a smuggled watch when you can get a world class Titan Quartz from Tata?
80% of the watches smuggled into India are fake or substandard. So should you still buy one when you know you may be cheated?
No longer do you need to risk buying a smuggled watch, or worry about the cost or inconvenience of repairing even a genuine import.
Now you can buy a world class watch from Tata: Titan Quartz. Choose from an international collection of over 350 fine quartz watches. From Rs. 380 onwards.
With Titan Quartz you have the Tata assurance of many years of faultless performance. And every watch is guaranteed for two years. Our after-sales network offers service with speed and economy. Battery replacement costs only Rs. 17 at authorised service centres.
With Titan Quartz, you'll never have to take any chances. Not ever.
Titan Quartz from Tata. The changing face of time.
* PRICES SHOWN ARE INCLUSIVE OF ALL LEVIES IN DELHI
Rs. 1007*
Rs. 1193*
Rs. 1050*
Rs. 1014*
Rs. 746*
Rs. 590*
Rs. 650*
Rs. 388*
Rs. 471*
TITAN
QUARTZ

Titan Quartz. The one gift that's always welcome.

The one gift that's right for any person, on any occasion. A Titan Quartz.

What makes Titan Quartz a wonderful gift is the joy with which it's received. And the pride with which it's always worn. Even if the recipient already owns a watch.

The fact is, times have changed. Just one watch is no longer enough – people wear different watches on different occasions, to suit different moods.

And Titan makes it easy for you to choose....with an international collection of over 400 fine quartz watches. Which means you'll find quite a few just right for each person you know.

What's more, Titan will soon introduce the "Titan Gift Voucher". It makes gifting a watch so simple, because it allows the person receiving the gift to make the choice.

The Tata assurance of reliability and a 2 year guarantee make Titan even more appealing. So if you're considering a gift, pick a Titan Quartz. No gift can be more certain to please.

Sleek and contemporary watch, with a unique offset second hand. For gents: Rs. 1155/-

Elegant dress watches: 10 micron, 18/23 carat duplex gold-plating. Studded with cubic Zirconia. Bangle bracelet hugs your wrist. For ladies Rs. 2495/- each.

The 5-dial multifunction watch shows time, day, date, month and the phases of the moon. Rs. 2431/-

An elegant watch, with gold dial and day/date display. For ladies Rs. 730/-

The Mariner. Made for sport and adventure. Tough, water-resistant upto 200m., with luminous dial and hands. Rs. 997/-

TITAN
QUARTZ
The Changing Face Of Time

*Prices inclusive of all levies in Maharashtra

Corporate Office: TITAN WATCHES LIMITED, Santa Towers, 71, Miller Road, Bangalore 560 052 Tel: 265051, 261321 **Regional Office:** TITAN WATCHES LIMITED, Holland House, 5. Bhagat Singh Marg, Colaba, Bombay 400 039 Tel: 2020019, 235056 **Titan Showrooms:** BOMBAY • Colaba Holland House, 5 Bhagat Singh Marg. • Dadar (W) 378, N C Kelkar Road, Opp Dadar Emporium Tel: 4226459 • Khar Silverstone, Linking Road. Tel: 6461620 • Thane Ram Niwas, Gokhale Rd, Naupada. Tel: 5361854 Or 5, 6, 6th floor, Jankalyan, Sector 98 • PUNE JM Road 1, Durga Chambers **Titan Shops:** BOMBAY Andheri (W) Kingston Apts, Shastri Nagar, Lokhandwala. • Borivli (W) Krishna Apts, Chandravarkar Road. Burholi Blcok A • Fort London Watch Co, Mahendra Chambers, 138 Dr DN Road. Girgaum S M Beharay & Co. Habib Bldg, Opp Girgaum Church Dadar (Central) Kumbar & Kamdar, Ambedkar Road. • Mulund (W) Khushro Apts. • Dadar TT Time Watch Makan, Empress Mahal Block A • Fort London Watch Co. Santa Cruz (W) J K Time, Sonapat Market, Station Road Krishna Watch Co., Arun Bazar, 2nd Hazaratbal Lane • Vasai Jan N Jon Anita Chambers, Antonii Road, Near UC • PUNE MG Road Butler Watch Co. • Bhandarkar Road Rayna Enterprises.

take care of the practical aspects of owning a timepiece. The 5Ps of the mix, therefore were:

The Product

* International styles, a wide range of 150 models.
* Modern, superior quartz technology.
* A 2 year (Tata) guarantee.

The Price

* Higher than existing Indian watches — clearly an in-built premium.
* Lower than foreign watches and those available at duty free shops.

The Place

This was Titan's most outstanding contribution to the Indian watch industry. It made shopping for watches a pleasant experience. Titan pioneered exclusive Titan showrooms — world class, modern, spacious — with a slick ambience having 'mood windows' for display, controlled lighting, granite finish, etc. In many ways, it was similar to "company showrooms" *à la* Raymonds.

The Promotion

This was one of the most visible faces of Titan. The innovative 'showcase' advertising in the print medium depicted the wide range. Prices placed alongside helped consumers 'shop' off the page. Remember, there was no 'internet' in those days!

The Positioning

"World class watches in a wide range of international styles, with the Tata guarantee of reliability and quality."

Just how well did this strategy work for Titan? Was the launch, so well-researched and timed, a smooth success? There seemed little reason that Titan should face any fight. But it did.

Titan 1988 — A case of unchanging consumer perceptions

Even post-entry, Titan did not have smooth going in the Indian market. The following perceptions were noted, after the Indian launch. Note how some reflect the strong entrenchment of HMT, while others are adverse reactions to the emotional qualities that Titan wanted to stand for!

* Titan is inferior to HMT, but is on par with Allwyn.
* It has a large variety for the upper class.
* It is a rich man's brand — for successful people!
* The Tata name is reassuring.
* It is of high quality and is attractive — however, it is not for the common man!

With the success of Titan had come another phenomenon: the proliferation of Indian made foreign quartz watches. Though these were not made by reputed companies and had limited and dated designs, they sold well because they were moderately priced. Given the fact that Titan had furthered the acceptability and the popularity of quartz movements, and the worldwide drop in their prices, these, as also the big players, were all now riding a wave. A wave created by Titan!

The way ahead... for all time

By 1988-89, post-entry, and even with slight superiority being established over HMT, Titan still faced an unexpected competitor, i.e., the smuggled product.

What could Titan do then? The lower end of the market continued to remain with the mechanical watches, or HMT. The upper end stayed with the imports. Titan could not afford to alienate the masses and yet had to also get shares from the top end of the market.

This was a clear case of being at risk by remaining stationary. At any time either end of the market could have competition entering, thereby eroding Titan's share. Titan needed to grow, but while

Ladies dress watch. Created to enhance formal wear. With delicately braided bracelet. 18 ct gold plating. Rs. 1074*

Next time he offers to buy you a saree, suggest Titan Quartz instead.

You probably own an array of beautiful sarees, and magnificent jewellery to go with them. But do you own a watch to complement your wardrobe? A fine quartz watch crafted for your wrist by Titan?

Choose from Titan's international collection of over 350 fine quartz watches. From just Rs. 380 to Rs. 2000.

Sleek and stylish like any watch you'd find overseas, Titan Quartz has the Tata assurance of faultless performance and is guaranteed for two years.

Titan Quartz requires no winding or resetting. Our widespread after-sales network offers service with speed and economy.

Titan Quartz : to go with any saree. And any occasion.

Rs. 1026*   Rs. 700*   Rs. 706*   Rs. 700*   Rs. 603*

TITAN
QUARTZ
The Changing Face Of Time

* PRICES SHOWN ARE INCLUSIVE OF ALL LEVIES IN MAHARASHTRA

CORPORATE OFFICE: Sona Towers, 71, Miller Road, Bangalore 560 052. Ph: 265051.

TITAN captures INDIA

|| Raga || A lyrical new range of watches for Indian women.

Raga captures Indian symbols, Ganesh, Surya, Lotus, and Indian motifs, Pochampalli, Bandhni, Lehariya...in a riot of rich, rangoli colours. 17 designs in all, to match a woman's every mood. And her wardrobe. Each Raga comes with 2 easily changeable straps. One to complement the dial, and the other, a neutral colour, to match any dress. Dial designs are available in limited numbers. (So, the moment you spot a Raga you like - buy it!)

In Raga, Titan has captured India, alive and vibrant. To win the hands of all Indian women.

NEW RAGA FROM TITAN

A Wardrobe For A Woman's Wrist

Rs. 1097*

Rs. 1097*

*Prices valid as on March 31, 1992 inclusive of all levies in Delhi

Available at all Titan Showrooms and other select outlets.

generating volumes, it could not be at the risk of compromising the long-term image that Titan wished to create.

Marketing strategy dictated that volumes would be generated only by developing new markets. To meet such threats, Titan began the process of developing new segments, each of which would later find a home in the consumer's mind.

Titan began targeting:

* The smuggled watches segment — the shift from wanting 'imported' to wanting a Titan.
* The mechanical segment, replacers and first-time buyers, many still uncomfortable with the idea of owning an expensive accessory.
* Gifting during weddings.
* The ladies segment.

From these needs were born the first of the many faces that Titan would launch — faces not only created from the distinctive individual dials, but faces that marked the different segments of India.

Reflecting the many faces of India...

Just how many different segments are there in a complex country teeming with millions? If the Titan faces were to mirror individual mindsets, be worn (or gifted) proudly as personal accessories, just how, which and where were these segments to be found, and then identified as those with the greatest potential? So, for the tradition-loving Indian woman, came *Raga*, a perfect accessory for her saris and salwars; then there was the elegantly plain *Exacta*, for the efficient professional, and then other faces were added slowly to the Titan repertoire.

Over the next couple of years, through 1992, Titan continued to focus on its basic premise for market expansion — promoting new ranges (and therefore, new buying segments) and promoting multiple ownership (sticking close to the "personal accessory" position). The latter was getting a further boost from research. Watches were a prized possession, as well as a prized gift. Indeed, gifting a watch was a position impossible to ignore. What's more, it was a position nobody could really claim. Again, it was a prime example of Titan leveraging one of its basic, original strengths.

...and the "other side of you"

To counter the threat of the low-priced, Indian made foreign quartzes, which promised the greatest volumes, Titan knew it had to provide an apt counter-product. How could it do so without jeopardising its image as one threatening the high-end imports? So Titan launched *Aqura,* to address the needs of the lowest end of the quartz spectrum, its low price and sporty style prompted by the worldwide success of *Swatch*. *Aqura* addressed the young (not the low price seekers!), and was launched with the dictum of "the other side of Titan, for the other side of you".

Such was its success in the market, that Titan decided to enter a tie-up with Timex to consolidate its position in this end of the market. This two-brand strategy had an impact on all of Titan's activities over the period of their alliance, i.e., from 1992 up to 1997, and marked one of their longest tie-ups, and greatest successes, a strategy worthy of study in its own right. Thanks to this soft, yet aggressive strategy of creating new fashion and style-based segments, Titan made its dent in the Indian market. It had, by now established the required changes in the Indian watch buying habits, and indeed, in the marketers' point of view:

* 50% of the watch market was the gifting segment.
* Marketing strategy was to explore the gifting segment.
* Success lay in expanding the product range; like the launch of *Aqura,* already done, there had to be more segments that were waiting to be explored.

Market Share Figures (1991-92)

Titan   57
HMT   27
Timex   0
IMFQ   16

Titan Sales 1991-92 (Primaries) — in lacs: Rs 21.76

Market Share Figures (1992-93)

Titan	56
HMT	23
Timex	3
IMFQ	18

Titan Sales 1992-93 (Primaries) — in lacs: Rs 24.75

But the brand was still in its infancy. Consumers had all the reasons to buy Titan, but besides being driven by advertising, it was a case of individuals having their own reasons. So just as consumers' need to gift watches was leading to the creation of the gifting concept in advertising, there was now the need to relook at what else the brand could stand for. Fortunately at this time new tools were available for brand equity management, and for finding new directions.

This reassessment now paved the way for the brand to grow now with a clear identity: *The (one who can lead to) affirmation of self-worth*. That this equity existed already in all aspects of the brand, and could be leveraged successfully for all aspects of advertising and also for driving its equity, was amply clear in the management of the brand over the coming years.

The affirmation of self-worth

Attitudinal statements eventually become the emotional glue that consumers identify with. If Titan was to tap into a huge Indian market, what attitude could its personality reflect? What would Titan stand for, that the consumer could identify with, and how could that attitude be taken forward for all time to come? This analysis became all the more important, given that in the first few years of its launch, Titan was merely presented as an international quality quartz watch. But the brand was under scrutiny for several reasons.

For one, the basic premise of offering an international quality quartz was completely devoid of emotional glue. The emotional glue lay in pride of ownership, and the joy of gifting, which is how the consumer identified with Titan. It was also the right time for brand evaluation, given the few years that the brand had already been in existence. Within its own story and through the consumer's approach to the brand, Titan could see an attitude emerge. How this was leveraged over time is a case of intelligent brand management.

This exercise, begun in 1994, used all the tools of brand management available at that time. Titan was evaluated against the newly available Hoefsteade. The core value of the product was recognised as the pride of ownership, and also of gifting, and the way Titan was fast emerging as the great Indian success story. Embedded into the Titan brand with conscious effort, was its cache — the symbol of esteem — whether for the wearer or as a gift, an affirmation of self-worth.

Also at hand was the recently developed Brand Print, the brand equity evaluation system of Ogilvy & Mather, the advertising agency for Titan. It, too, confirmed a similar pattern. Titan was definitely seen as an innovator, liked because it represented self-worth, and chosen because it met the underlying human need for taking pride in all activities. Thus, the Titan attitude claimed:

> "I am what I am because of what I have made of myself. Wearing a Titan is a true affirmation of my self-worth because what drives me also drives Titan — an inner strength, the ability to achieve and to innovate in a world that has forgotten how to."
>
> "Titan is a proud brand and so am I."

While this was entrenched into the core of the brand, Titan took this self-worth forward at all levels of activity.

In all its many Ps of marketing, the reflecting of self-worth shines through. This was seen in the way the product was presented in showrooms, in its advertising (whether Indianised or Westernised), or in its advertising imagery. In creating new products and lines, this attitude of achievement and innovation, too, was inherent. It was the only way ahead given the fact that Titan was competing, eventually, with all the watches in the world!

When Titan wished to pre-empt the challenge posed by international brands, which were poised to enter the fast liberalising country, this affirmation of self-worth again expressed itself. Titan became the first Indian watch manufacturer to enter the world market. And all on its own strength. So much so, it didn't even try to push its upper-end ranges (e.g., *Tanishq*) into the international markets. It was the core brand that was made to compete. A case of having inner strength, of being the innovator, the proud international Indian! A triumphant reaffirmation of self-worth!

Driving the market

Saying it with watches...

With its twin objectives set in place Titan began its aggressive push. Over the next few years came the advertising campaigns that promoted a watch as the ideal gift. Gifting as an advertising theme had already been done in the earlier years, but never with such deliberation. (Interestingly, even though Titan used festivals for its theme of gifting, it also created attractive reasons for purchase at festival time. Never was Titan sold at a discount or a sale, except at the time of a festival or the new year. Such has been the finesse of Titan's discounting, that it has never been perceived as a discounted brand!)

While some occasions were necessarily personal (such as the anniversary in the restaurant), there were others that had definitely more mass appeal — gifting on festivals, for your nearest kin (from the man to his wife, on Diwali), etc. Years later the festival gift route went on to include Onam, Durga Puja, Teacher's Day, young lovers in a library, and even the thief who leaves untouched a ready-to-be-gifted Titan on a table.

Market Share Figures (1993-94)

Titan	52
HMT	13
Timex	19
IMFQ	16

Titan Sales 1993-94 (Primaries) — in lacs: Rs 26.20

Saying it to many ...

The other twin driver for market expansion was to appeal to the many segments in the Indian market. With *Aqura* had begun the process of moving away from the Titan name, and moving into different segments. It was clear that "*Aqura,* from Titan" could work well with other segments as well. Also in fashion were steel watches for the no-nonsense precisionist, or the delicate pieces (almost jewellery) for the fashion model (or the aspirant), or the range for the top end executive, or even that for the art gallery enthusiast's casual, yet formal, evenings. Of course, the most well-known of this strategy was that done for *Raga*. This was perhaps the first instance where a fashion accessory completely ignored the male segment, and tapped into their better halves! The other well-known Titan offspring is *Tanishq* — watches that begin to retail in five figures, and are sold only through still more exclusive showrooms, if not jewellery stores.

Market Share Figures (1994-95)
Titan   46
HMT   09
Timex   23
IMFQ   22
Titan Sales 1994-95 (Primaries) — in lacs: Rs 29.87

Market Share Figures (1995-96)
Titan   39
HMT   07
Timex   24
IMFQ   30
Titan Sales 1995-96 (Primaries) — in lacs: Rs 33.68

Watch out, it's time for innovations!

With time, all of Titan's innovations have had to answer two critical questions:

* Do they continue to establish Titan as an innovator of superior technological products?

New! Aqura from Titan. Get ready to get noticed

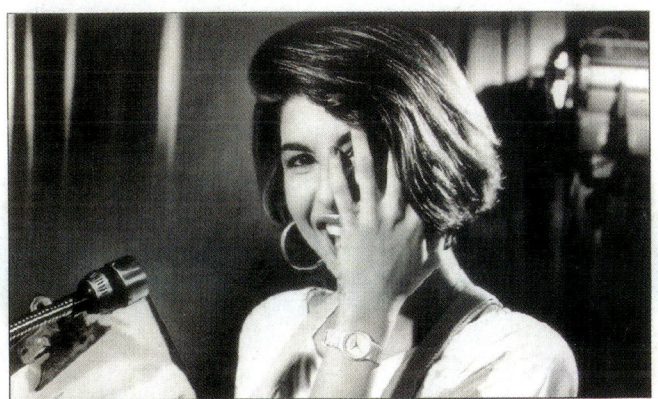

Put an Aqura on your wrist. And take centre stage.

Aqura is the new range in Titan's international collection of fine quartz watches: contemporary, bold, distinctive.

The looks range from the vibrantly colourful and sportily luminous to those with neo-classical flair. Rugged and water-resistant, an Aqura is ready to go anywhere.

With over one hundred designs to choose from, you'll find it easy to pick at least one that's right for you. And Aqura's price tag is as surprising as its looks: from Rs.370 to Rs.450.

Aqura comes with the Tata assurance of reliability *and* a 2 year guarantee.

Aqura is everything you'd expect a Titan to be. Wear one. You'll get used to the attention.

TITAN
QUARTZ
aqura

Born of the spirit to defy the elements. The will to survive. And to Never give up.

There's a lot to learn from a watch.

At freezing, treacherous altitudes there are only some things you can hang on to. Guts, courage and Titan PSI 2000. Armoured steel body. Screw-in-crown for 100m water resistance. Unidirectional timer ring. Luminous markings.

TITAN psi 2000

Geared for the next level of sport.

Prices range from Rs. 1695 to Rs. 7400.

* Do they address a new range of people (and hence build strong emotional bonds with the consumer)?

The latest launches continue to focus on these aspects, enhancing the premium image of Titan and also its credibility as an innovator:

Insignia - 1996
Slim - 1997
PSI 2000 - 1997

Similarly, as the competition came in from the lowest ends of the price segment, and as the lucrative market for alarm clocks began to grow, Titan:

* successfully launched *Sonata* — low-priced watches,
* entered the clocks segment with the launch of basic and premium clocks,
* continued to advertise to promote gifting,
* continued showcasing of product and festival advertising.

Market Share Figures (1996-97)
Titan   36
HMT   08
Timex   22
IMFQ   34
Titan Sales 1996-97 (Primaries) — in lacs: Rs 33.99

Market Share Figures (1997-98)
Titan   38
HMT   07
Timex   21
IMFQ   34
Titan Sales 1997-98 (Primaries) — in lacs: Rs 39.60

Market Share Figures (1998-99)
Titan   43
HMT   08
Timex   16
IMFQ   33
Titan Sales 1998-99 (Primaries) — in lacs: Rs 47.10

Today

The latest Titan strategy extends to more segments, and so to greater expansion and penetration of the markets. So, year 2000 has seen the launch of *Fastrack* (for youth), *Dash* (for children), *Nebula* (for the business class), and *Regalia*. Already, *Dash* has become a runaway success, even before the media blitz. Digital watches, introduced in 1999 for the youth, have also been a great success. *Nebula*, priced between Rs 5,950–Rs 32,000 has already reached a position of demand outstripping supply.

By all accounts, and after 10 years, the Titan strategy has outlined the correct way for pushing a mass brand. A quick look at the brand reveals the following:

Titan has changed the structure of the watch market

As mentioned, by merely defining the product as a personal accessory, rather than as a timepiece, Titan has been able to keep on re-inventing its products, and therefore, redefining its markets.

Increased market size and share

Again, thanks to looking at its product differently, Titan has been able to constantly create a need for it amongst differing niches, without sacrificing its core commitment.

Tremendous muscle in retail, an entry barrier
to international competition

The Titan Showroom has become a landmark on our cities' streets. How many other brands can claim that? Within 10 years of its inception? Today any mass entrant to India in the same category would find it extremely difficult to match its quality of distribution. Those who tied up with Titan (à la Timex) have benefited the most!

Advertising is consistent and credible,
faithful to the brand values and personality

Mozart's Ninth Symphony is now better known as the signature tune of Titan watches and this has remained consistent since the beginning. Every gifting story captures a slice of life. New ranges are showcased through clear definition.

*Constantly creating excitement and
addressing new segments with new launches*

The slimmest watch, the first chronograph, the first teen quartz — there are few, worldwide, who can compete with such a range of innovations as Titan. All along, they have been consolidating their original image as the innovator (from the time they began by competing with HMT), and as the trend and technology leader. They have also made themselves the first stop for the multiple product user, or gifter.

Conclusion

There is no question that Titan today is a successful branding story. I feel quite strongly that Titan watches should always retain the 'Titan' name on the dial. I am not sure as to what extent the brand image of Titan has been enhanced by the introduction of *Tanishq*. However, what further action Titan should take to consolidate its position as the leader-innovator, so as to increase not only the total watch market, but also its market share, is a subject for future discussion.

7

POWER OF BRAND EQUITY — BRAND EXTENSION

Introduction

What is Brand Equity? These two words are being used extensively, particularly in recent years in the corporate world. Brand Equity signifies a set of assets linked to a brand's name and symbol, that adds to the value provided by a product or service to a company and/or to a company's clients. The major assets consist of:

(1) **Brand Name Awareness.** This refers to the strength of the brand's presence in the consumer's mind.
(2) **Perceived Quality.** In fact, the perceived quality is usually at the heart of what the consumer is buying. It, in a way, gives the brand its identity.
(3) **Brand Loyalty.** A brand's value is largely created by the consumer loyalty it commands.

No wonder therefore that there is such a fascination with brands. Brands create trust, and trust is the precondition to loyalty. Ultimately it is loyalty that delivers continuous business to the company that owns those brands.

One of the ways a company derives substantial benefit from a well-established brand is by brand extension of that brand equity. Sometimes that extension is created just for reaping the benefit of the brand equity in a related product category, to add extra business, and of course, profit. In some instances that extension turns out to be, both from the point of volume sale and profit, a bigger success than the mother brand. However, it is a double-edged sword. If, for some reason, that extended brand turns out to be a failure, then it can adversely affect the mother brand.

Also, there must be synergy between the products, in order to get the maximum benefit out of brand extension. It is essential that the 'core' value of the brand be maintained. For example, when Beecham decided to extend the *Horlicks* brand, it made sure that the new products in essence were offering the same core value — in this case 'nourishment' — in all their new products.

Once a brand has been established, such extension can be particularly beneficial, if the target customers happen to be the same. This is understandable, since the brand is already well-known to the target customers, they will automatically have enough faith to try out the new brand-extended product. And if the new product delivers what it promises, chances are that the customer will become a loyal user of this new product as well. This is the new benefit the company will reap from having established the original mother brand.

Brand Extension — the Real Winner

MAGGI

Sometimes, having established a brand, the company may find that in the ultimate analysis the company is not making the money that it had originally targetted. What should it do then? Abandon the brand, or carry on slogging, or, better still, investigate whether there is a possibility for extending the brand in an area, where, if the extended brand becomes a success, the company will be able to make money. In other words, should the company try to derive the benefit from all the hard work done to establish a particular brand by extending the brand in some other area, where it sees an opportunity to make further money. In short, derive the maximum benefit from having established the brand.

Nestlé did exactly that with one of their brands — *Maggi*. It is indeed a fascinating case study.

Background

Maggi, as a brand, has been known in the market, particularly in the western world, for quite some time as the maker of Bouillon or Soup Cubes. In fact, when Nestlé decided to introduce *Maggi* in India, it started by introducing the Bouillon Cube.

In 1974 the company introduced *Maggi* bouillon in Kerala, as a 'test marketing' operation. The initial result was not encouraging. Having then realised that maybe the dietary habits of Keralites are not conducive to the idea of drinking soup at a meal, the company decided to extend the distribution of this product to Goa. It was argued that since Goan food habits have some similarity with western habits they may take to having soup with their meals. Fortunately for the company, its analysis turned out to be more or less correct. *Maggi* soup cubes became a success in a limited way, and still is.

There is one other point. The flavour of soup cubes jells well with non-vegetarian food, but since the majority of Indians are

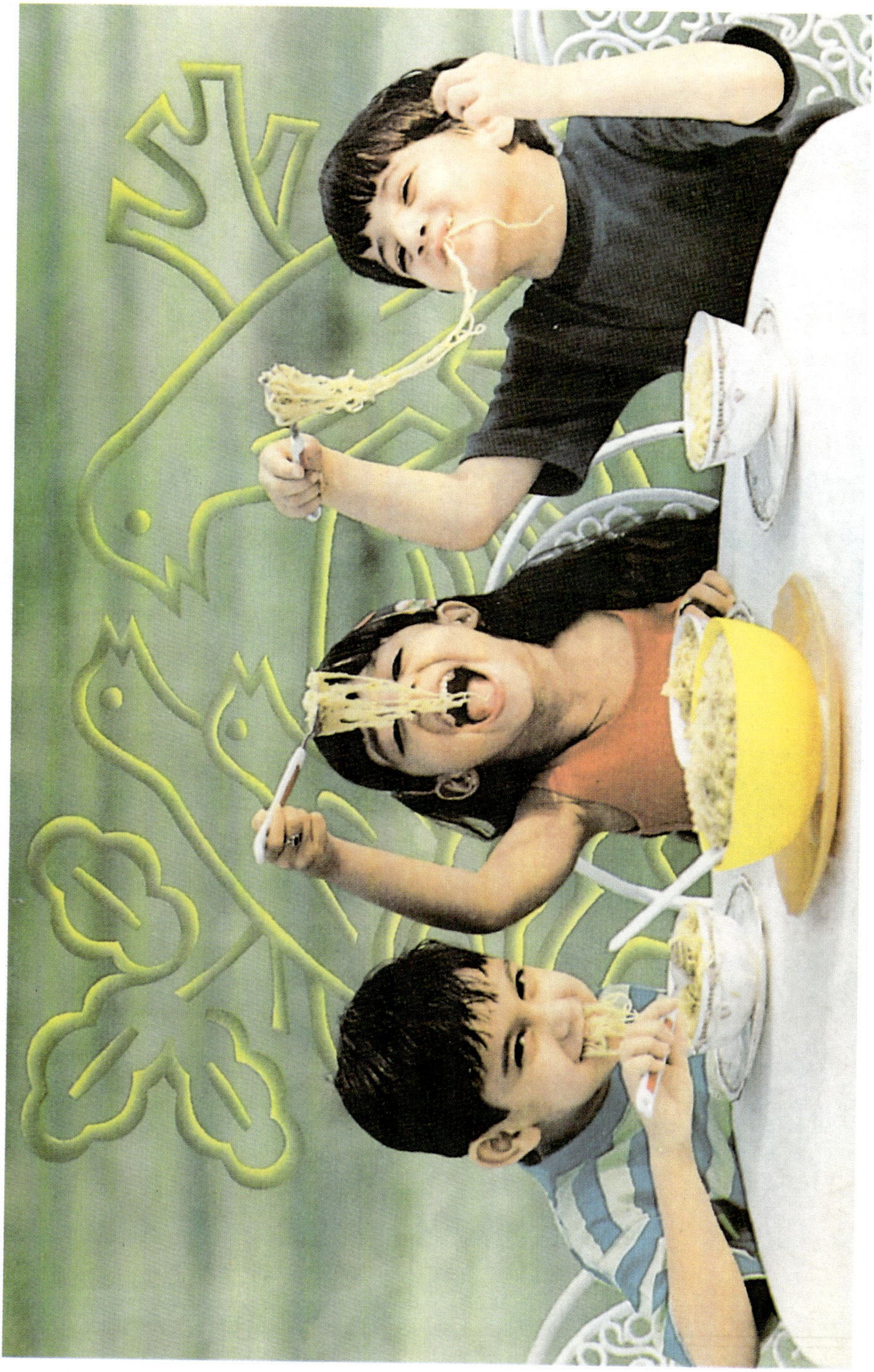

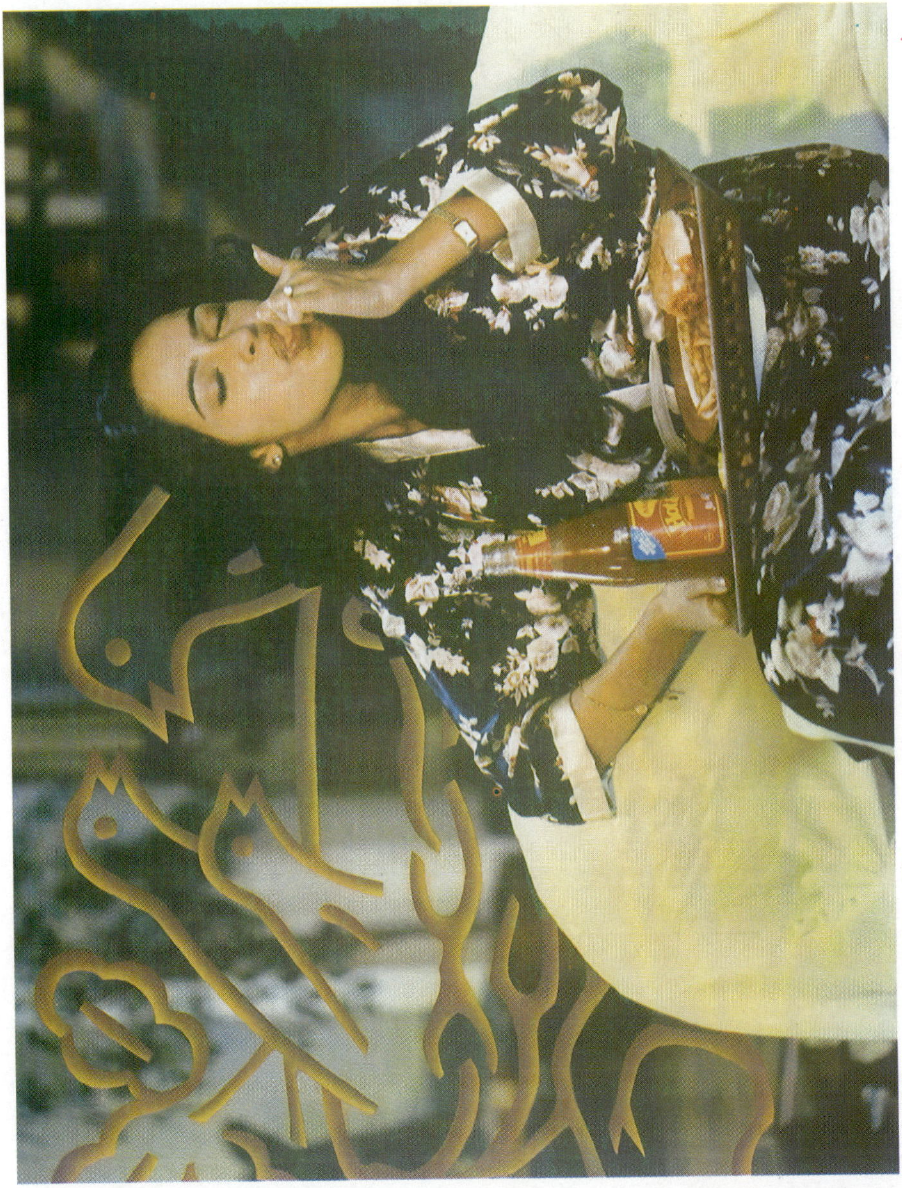

vegetarians, the company realised that *Maggi* soup cubes would therefore take time to be a big seller. They thus, decided to wait for sometime before further extension.

Maggi 2-Minute Noodles

In the meantime, Nestlé looked at the snack market, as did many other companies in the early '80s. Traditionally Indians are very fond of 'samosas' and 'kachoris' with their tea and coffee. Branded potato chips had also started appearing, though not in a big way. But, Nestlé looked at this market, in a different way. They thought of, what may be termed, 'niche' marketing — Children's Snacks. There were two distinct advantages they visualised in entering this segment. These were:

(1) At that time, there were no special products or brands, specifically addressed to this market.
(2) There existed a specific need for a product for school-returning children.

The company realised that whatever product they finally choose must have the following ingredients:

* It must be wholesome, as well as liked by children.
* It must be ready, or could be made ready in a matter of minutes.

Thus was born the idea of a '2-minute' noodle. Nestlé knew that there existed a 'noodle' market, particularly in the East, mainly due to the existence of a Chinese population, but no product or brand at that time, satisfied the above two needs. At that point there was no brand or product which catered specifically for the children's market.

Product proposition

Nestlé, therefore, finally launched their 2-minutes Noodle, with the brand name *Maggi* in 1983. Two salient points the company stressed in their communication were:

(1) It is meant for children — the product is wholesome and tasty.
(2) It is quick and convenient to make — hence the words '2-minutes'.

Obviously the communication was addressed both to the user, i.e., children; and to the decision maker, i.e., mothers. The brand proposition was therefore:

* fast to cook,
* good to eat.

In order to build good volume, Nestlé decided to price it comparatively cheap, i.e., Rs. 2.40 per packet of 100gm. And Nestlé followed the golden rule of brand-building: be consistent with your ad message. Throughout the brand's advertising campaign, Nestlé stuck to its original message—be it visual, press or any other media.

You and Maggi make a 'tastier meal'

Sales volume and profitability

The brand was a success. At the end of 2 years, volume sale was approximately 4000 tons with a value of approximately Rs. 9 crores. In the '80s, by any standard, it was a very good sale. However, because of the pricing strategy adopted by the company, and the money they had spend to build the brand, Nestlé did not make any money.

Over the next few years, Nestlé tried to gradually increase the price, taking into account inflation, as well as an improvement in the margin, without in any way jeopardising volume sale. At the end of 10 years, volume sale increased to approximately 6000 tons; value sale: Rs. 25 crores. Although the packet was then selling at Rs. 7/-, Nestlé still did not make much money.

Brand Extension

MAGGI KETCHUP & SAUCES

By the time the 2-minute noodle was firmly establishing the brand 'Maggi', Nestlé was working on a brand extension in an area where they thought they might be able to leverage the brand, and make some money also this time. They decided to enter the Ketchup market with the brand 'Maggi'. Finally in 1985, when *Maggi Noodle*, had already notched a 4000 ton business (that's a lot of 100gm packets); and, thus ensured the establishment of the brand 'Maggi', Nestlé launched their *Maggi Ketchup*.

At that time the total market for ketchup was approximately 4000 tons, and the brand leader was Kisan which held approximately 65 per cent of the market. There were, of course, a large number of local brands. Kisan sold its ketchup in 500gm bottles.

When Nestlé decided to enter this market, it decided upon a 400gm bottle to give the consumer a 'price-point' advantage. The company also decided to launch the product simultaneously in 80 cities of the country, virtually an all-India launch. The main talking point of their advertising was, "What Ketchup does to your food": tasty and more palatable. It was really a clever move because it paved the way for subsequent additions, such as:

* Tomato Chilli, i.e., Hot and sweet,
* Masala Chilli,
* Chilli Garlic.

These additions made a point of difference against competitors' Tomato Ketchup. One cannot forget the message carried in the ad:
Enjoy the difference

Volume Sale and Profitability

In 1999, when the total ketchup market had exceeded 16000 tons, Nestlé was the brand leader with approximately 48 per cent of the market. Not only had the brand helped to increase the total market, but it had also taken over the leadership of the market.

What is perhaps even more satisfying to Nestlé is that the 'Maggi' brand has now become a profitable brand. Thus the investment that Nestlé put in, for establishing the 'Maggi' brand through its 2-minute noodles, paid handsome dividends, through its extension in *Maggi* ketchup and sauces.

Postscript

One of the main reasons why the brand name 'Maggi' helped in the success of *Maggi* ketchup and sauces, is the fact that the target customer, both for the 2-minute noodles and *Maggi* sauces are the same, i.e., mother and housewife. As stated earlier, with a sale of 6000 tons (100gm pkts.), of 2-minute noodles, the brand name 'Maggi' had already been established in the mind of the target customers, long before *Maggi* ketchup and sauces were introduced. Naturally therefore when the new product appeared in the market, the housewife was already convinced about the quality/price of the new product, and was therefore willing to try out the product. And, of course, the efficient and well-oiled distribution system that Nestlé has in India makes sure that the new brand is available at all the outlets from where the housewife normally buys her requirements. The fact that she can now buy variations in terms of other sauces made it even more attractive for the housewife who could now indulge in buying more than one bottle of ketchup for the household.

Here then is a perfect example of a brand, where extensions helped in giving the company returns for the investment it made on the mother brand. This, ultimately, is the power of 'Brand Equity'.

Brand Extension — The Key to Volume Sale

DETTOL

Background

[Dettol ↑ Protects]

Dettol was first used in a leading UK maternity hospital in the early 1930s and played a major role in reducing by half the mortality rate in women suffering from puerperal fever. Shortly thereafter in 1933, with the endorsement of the medical profession, *Dettol* was launched to the general public. *Dettol's* fame spread even more with the Second World War during which, along with sulphonamide drugs, it played a major part in the marked reduction of wound sepsis. It was carried by many troops as a wound disinfectant from as far as Dunkirk to Rangoon. So vital was *Dettol's* part in the war that the production facility was swiftly moved from its location in Hull (UK) which was ravaged by bombings to the more peaceful Yorkshire Dales.

In fact, the naming of the product had an interesting angle. The name *Dettol* was chosen as it conveyed no particular meaning or idea and there were no preconceived notions as to the nature of the product. However, the name did seem to have a medical flavour.

Ever since its introduction more than 65 years ago, *Dettol* has become one of the world's most widely used and trusted antiseptics. Its popularity today extends to more than a 100 countries across the globe, and more than a billion people on our planet have heard of it. Over the years extensive clinical studies and laboratory tests have shown *Dettol* to be highly effective against microbes, yet gentle on the skin.

In India also, *Dettol* has been at the forefront of providing the best in antiseptic protection for our people, in order to help them improve the quality of their families' health and hygiene. Research has shown that *Dettol* has a strong heritage and occupies a unique position of trust and reliability in the consumer's mind. Consumers have described *Dettol* as the 'king of germkill' and, for many people it is the first thing that comes to mind on getting a cut or a wound. It is a brand which offers a set of both rational and emotional benefits to consumers, who therefore perceive *Dettol* as being a 'Doctor Friend' to their families. Many people continue to recall with nostalgia the 'letter' film campaign of *Dettol*, which showed a mother reading a letter from her son, who is away at boarding school, and how she felt reassured that her son who was away from home was safe with the protection of *Dettol*.

Dettol Liquid

Liquid *Dettol* is today synonymous with the liquid antiseptic market. It commands a market share of 83.5% of this market. *Savlon*, which was re-launched by Johnson & Johnson in 1993, only has 13.5%. In fact, the history of *Savlon* shows that even when the brand was owned by ICI in the past, its share was more or less the same. Although Johnson & Johnson pumped in a lot of money, (almost the same as that allocated to *Dettol*), to re-launch the brand, it has not been able to make a dent in the share of *Dettol* liquid. Such is the strength of the *Dettol* Brand Equity. The total market however, is relatively small — approximately Rs. 65 crores.

Constraints

Inspite of having such a strong Brand Equity, there were however two main constraints from the profit point of view. They were:

(1) **Price Control:** *Dettol* falls under the government's rule of price control for certain drugs.
(2) **Restricted Volume Sale:** By the very nature of the usage of the product — both in terms of frequency and volume used on each application — even when the penetration of the product is high, the volume sale is rather limited. The total antiseptic liquid market is only Rs. 65 crores. Reckitt & Colman, therefore started looking at the opportunity the very strong brand equity *Dettol* provides for brand extension. Finally in 1979/80, the company launched *Dettol Soap*.

[**Dettol**®]

Strong enough to protect the ones you love...

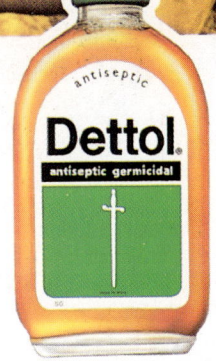

For times when no ordinary bath will do.

The 100% bath

DETTOL SOAP

The initial launch was not much of a success. While analysing the results, after due market research, the company realised that they had positioned *Dettol Soap* on the wrong platform. When they analysed the success of the mother brand, i.e., *Dettol* Liquid, the company realised that the brand had been promoted, over the years, on a dual platform:

(1) Emotional: i.e., 'love and care' — Mother's love and care in treating any wound suffered by a loved one.
(2) Functional: i.e., antiseptic. The product in fact delivered what it promised — it is definitely antiseptic and cured the wound.

If one analyses the above two platforms, it will be evident that really speaking the brand equity of *Dettol* is antiseptic protection, and that:

(1) it is effective; and
(2) it is a tried and trusted product.

In their communication, the company had stressed only the first platform, i.e., 'love and care'. When you think about it, one realises that for a product like soap, this particular platform does not quite fit in with the general antiseptic platform, i.e., antiseptic protection. No wonder then that the new product did not meet with much success.

There was one other factor, which the research results pointed out. Even before the introduction of *Dettol Soap*, there was evidence that some of the consumers were in fact using *Dettol* liquid in a diluted form in their bath water (in a bucket). In fact such usage was also seen in the case of shaving water as well.

Thus was born the idea of the 100% bath. That is the way, the company brought in the functional aspect, i.e., the 'antiseptic' platform. Fortunately for the company, the second launch, or rather the re-launch of *Dettol Soap* in 1982/83 coincided with the overwhelming feeling of many consumers that the air is polluted with dust and germs, and therefore you need more than a simple bath — you need a really 'clean clean' bath — hence, you need a 100% bath. Consumers understood the meaning of this 100% bath idea.

This became clearly evident from the sales figures right from 1982 till today. Over the years, not only have volume sales improved year by year, but the brand share has also improved continuously. Today, *Dettol Soap* is the number 2 brand (after *Liril*) in the premium soap market, notching up a 10 per cent share of this segment. That, in fact, is quite a volume, since the bath soap market is a huge one — 80,000 tons valued at Rs. 1400 crores. In fact, during the same period, almost all the major brands have lost their share of the market. *Dettol Soap* has won this share of the market, with a comparatively lesser share of the voice! That's what a strong Brand Equity does for your business.

Dettol Plaster

One other market the company looked at was medicated plaster. This was a Rs. 55 crore market, and *Band-Aid* was the brand leader, with 60% of the market, although *Handyplast* was also a major player with a 20% share. However, *Handyplast* appeared to have achieved their share mainly through below-the-line activities. At present *Dettol Plaster* has 12 per cent of the market. The company realises that although the concept of '*Dettol* protection' does fit in very nicely with this product, in order to dislodge the brand leader *Band-Aid*, it would require a fair amount of investment both in terms of money and effort. Also, since the product was contract manufactured, the company has been experiencing supply constraints. For the time being therefore they would rather concentrate on brands which give them bigger volumes, and come back to this brand at a later stage.

Dettol Shaving Cream

One other product that the company launched, piggy-backing on the *Dettol* Brand Equity is *Dettol* Shaving Cream, in 1998. It was mentioned earlier that *Dettol* liquid has often been used in shaving water. The introduction of this product is really an extension of that concept. The shaving cream market is relatively small, approximately Rs. 80 crores. Within a short period, this product has notched up a brand share of 6.5 per cent.

Fresh Fragrance

Dettol®
SHAVING CREAM

Dettol Protects

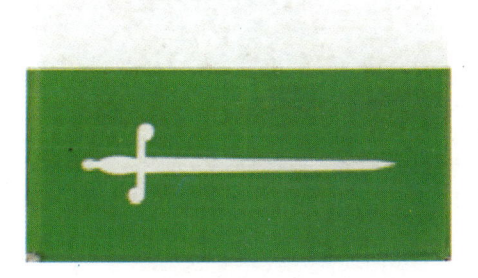

MALTED FOOD
(Proprietary Food)

MADE IN INDIA BY
SMITHKLINE BEECHAM
CONSUMER HEALTHCARE LTD.
NABHA-147 201

Under licence from
HORLICKS LIMITED, U.K.
(Proprietors of the Trade Mark 'Horlicks')
THROUGH SMITHKLINE BEECHAM ASIA LTD

NET WT. 500g

BEST BEFORE WITHIN 12 MONTHS FROM THE DATE OF PACKAGING.

M.R.P.: Rs.
(incl. of all taxes)
PKD.:
B.No.:

For any query or suggestion, write to:
SB Consumer Services
P.O. Box 122, New Delhi 110 001.

SB SmithKline Beecham

NEW SMART NUTRIENTS™ Horlicks

New Horlicks is now enriched with SMART NUTRIENTS™ – nutrients which have been scientifically researched and proven to be essential for mental and physical development.

Along with the other vital nutrients present in Horlicks, SMART NUTRIENTS™ are essential to help keep your family mentally sharp and physically active. Making New Horlicks the smart choice of a smart family.

New Horlicks is made by a unique process that seals in the natural goodness of wheat, milk and malted barley into an appetising and easily digestible drink.

3 STEPS TO A NOURISHING AND DELICIOUS DRINK

Take three heaped teaspoonfuls of Horlicks (27g) in a cup.

Add a little hot (not boiling) water or milk and stir to make a paste.

Stirring briskly, slowly add hot water or milk as desired. Add sugar to taste.

NEW SMART NUTRIENTS™
Horlicks
nourishing food drink
Elaichi
The Great Nourisher

NUTRITION FACTS

NUTRIENTS	% DAILY REQUIRE- MENT*	BENEFIT
Folate	100	**SMART NUTRIENTS™** A synergistic combination – to help keep you mentally sharp and alert, physically active.
Vitamin B6	100	
Vitamin B12	100	
Vitamin C	133	
Vitamin B2	100	
Iron	100	
Iodine	50	Adequate mental development.
Zinc	15	Healthy immune system.
Calcium	50	Strong bones. Strong teeth.
Vitamin A	50	Good vision; healthy skin.
Vitamin D	50	Absorption of calcium for stronger bones.
Vitamin B1	50	Release of energy from food; healthy heart.
Niacin	50	healthy nervous system.
Protein	NS	Healthy growth and development; tissue repair.
Carbohydrate	NS	Energy
Fat	NS	Energy

INGREDIENTS
Wheat Flour, Milk Solids, Malted Barley, Malt Extract, Sugar, Minerals, Vitamins, Cardamom Powder.

CONTAINS ADDED FLAVOURS

ADDED NUTRIENTS PER 100 g
370mcg Folate, 3.7mg Vitamin B6, 1.85mcg Vitamin B12, 148mg Vitamin C, 2.36mg Vitamin B2, 25.9mg Iron

*In 2 servings as per CODEX Alimentarius Commission of the WHO/FAO, 1995.

Horlicks Brand Extension

ELAICHI HORLICKS

When I joined HMM (now SmithKline Beecham) back in mid-'72, *Horlicks* was their only product — but a product which had tremendous Brand Equity. I realised quite soon that there was a primary and overriding need to diversify and introduce other products, or more precisely other brands. Unfortunately there were constraints in terms of the company's manufacturing license (remember the 'license raj' before liberalization!), and therefore the type of product/products we could conceivably develop at that point of time.

One of the best ways, I thought, that we could diversify was to undertake brand extensions. In other words, why not make use of the tremendous Brand Equity of *Horlicks*. Thus was born the idea of flavoured *Horlicks*. A lot of research was conducted to gauge the acceptance of the right flavour.

Elaichi was chosen from among the 3 flavours which were researched by IMRB and it emerged as a clear winner on dimensions of taste and aroma, thickness and sweetness. The three flavours were Elaichi, Almond and Saunf. It was evident that all three flavours were distinctly Indian and traditionally associated in this country with health benefits, besides being ingredients within the Ayurvedic system of medicine. Incidentally we did research other 'western' flavours like Vanilla, Strawberry, and Banana, none of which came near to the acceptance level of Elaichi.

Marketing Strategy

The main aims and objectives of the company's strategy and the philosophy behind the *Elaichi Horlicks* launch was as follows:

* To introduce a second line of products to the existing standard *Horlicks*.

* Using the constraints of the existing license to give such a product a distinct image of its own.
* To strengthen company sales in the North and West zones which were traditionally weak markets for the company in that these markets were perceived as having negatives on the taste and flavour dimensions. *Elaichi Horlicks* was therefore introduced in the North and West to fulfil the following requirements:

    (a) A somewhat negative image of standard *Horlicks* on the grounds of taste and flavour had to be overcome, including its image as a medically promoted product (at that time).

    (b) It therefore had to be seen as a milk additive full of taste and flavour and therefore as a substitute to the brown milkfoods rather than to standard *Horlicks* (to avoid cannibalisation).

    (c) Its image needed to be modern, as opposed to the so-called old-fashioned, traditional *Horlicks*.

It was perceived that the above objectives could be met by prefixing *Horlicks* with the word 'Elaichi' and using the whole word 'Elaichi Horlicks' as the brand. The colour of the label was changed to a fresh green and the word 'new' inserted to give it a modern image. The advertising slogan carried the promise of "doubles the nourishment of milk", through which it was hoped that the targeted group would perceive the new product as a milk additive, which is precisely what the North and West markets are all about — markets where brown powders are added to milk to give taste and flavour.

Test markets and results

The product was test marketed in Pune (West zone). Three months after the launch, research was conducted to find out the acceptability of the product. Its launch was successful in that its objectives were fulfilled; the advertising was also effective in convincing the consumers of the theme message. Initial product acceptance was indeed good.

Elaichi Horlicks was perceived as a flavoured drink by the targeted group. The slogan "doubles the nourishment of milk" underscored its usage as a milk additive and research pointed out that the manner of usage of *Elaichi Horlicks* was in milk or in a mixture of milk and water — the bulk of *Elaichi Horlicks* buyers were *Bournvita* users.

Follow-up position

However, we noticed that sales were distinctly dropping off. Further research confirmed our lurking doubt about the Elaichi flavour and its acceptance by consumers over an extended period of time. In other words, flavour fatigue sets in for a flavour like Elaichi.

The then-current position

Elaichi Horlicks was fully launched in the North and West markets. Although *Elaichi Horlicks* has limited sales (frequency and intensity of sales among users being low), it is still satisfying a particular need of the market. Even though the company has discontinued product advertising, *Elaichi Horlicks* is still making a fair contribution to the profit of the company. As of now, the company sells *Elaichi Horlicks* as a flavour variant to standard Horlicks.

Conclusion

In retrospect, in 'taste' oriented products, it may be advisable to have a prolonged 'test' marketing period. Also 'tracking' type of research needs to be conducted to find out to what extent the new product is able to satisfy the most important element of Brand Asset, i.e., brand loyalty.

Brand Extension

HORLICKS BISCUITS

After the successful introduction of *Boost*, HMM was still looking for a product which could successfully capitalise on the strength of the *Horlicks* brand as a Brand Extension. One such product HMM thought about was *Horlicks Biscuits*. Unfortunately at that time there existed an agreement with Britannia Biscuits, as a result of which HMM was required to sell *Horlicks* to Britannia Biscuits, who in turn would produce and sell *Horlicks Biscuits*.

As the date of expiry of that agreement approached, HMM decided:

(1) To terminate the agreement on the appointed date; and
(2) To launch *Horlicks Biscuits*.

Why *Horlicks* Biscuits

Apart from the fact that *Horlicks Biscuits* would be able to benefit immensely from the strength of the *Horlicks* Brand Equity, it would be a fit case for extension of that brand because of the following reasons:

(1) It would be assured of deriving the benefits of Brand Loyalty. After all, it is on the strength of customer loyalty that a brand draws its strength. Since *Horlicks* is a household name in the South and East, bulk of the users of *Horlicks* will almost automatically become users of *Horlicks Biscuits*.

(2) With the distribution strength of *Horlicks*, *Horlicks Biscuits* would be made available at all suitable outlets. In India the key to the success of a fast-moving consumer product, I believe, is distribution. In recent years, whenever a successful multinational like Kelloggs, Heinz, etc., wanted to come to India, the first thing they wanted to talk about was distribution. After all, depending on the type of product, the company may have to stock anywhere between 100,000 to 300,000 outlets.

RICH IN CALCIUM
Horlicks
BISCUITS
NOW!
MORE
NUTRITIOUS
MILK
Horlicks

SB
NEW
Junior
Horlicks
nourishing food drink
The Great Nourisher for 1-2-3 year olds

NUTRITION FACTS
NUTRIENTS
% DAILY REQUIREMENT*
BENEFIT
Folate 100
Vitamin B6 100
Vitamin B12 100
Vitamin C 125
Vitamin B2 100
Iron 100
+A unique scientific combination – essential for mental and physical development.
Iodine 50 Adequate mental development.
Zinc 20 Healthy immune system.
Calcium 50 Strong bones. Strong teeth.
Vitamin A 50 Good vision; healthy skin.
Vitamin D 50 Absorption of calcium for stronger bones.
Vitamin B1 50 Release of energy from food; healthy heart;
Niacin 50 healthy nervous system.
Vitamin E 50 Maintenance of body tissues.
Vitamin K 50 Healthy blood clotting.
Protein NS Healthy growth and development; tissue repair.
Carbohydrate NS Energy
Fat NS Energy
ADDED NUTRIENTS PER 100g
100mcg Folate, 2mg Vitamin B6, 1.4mcg Vitamin B12, 100mg Vitamin C, 1.6mg Vitamin B2, 20mg Iron.
INGREDIENTS
Milk Solids, Wheat Flour, Malted Barley, Sugar, Malt Extract, Minerals, Vitamins and Vanilla Flavour.
CONTAINS ADDED FLAVOUR
Not suitable for infants below one year of age.
*In 2 serves as per US RDA - National Research Council, 1989.
SB
NEW
Junior
Horlicks
nourishing food drink
The Great Nourisher for 1-2-3 year olds
NEW
Junior
Horlicks
Children between 1 and 3 need special nourishment for healthy growth.
They can, however, be fussy eaters.
New Junior Horlicks, along with other vital nutrients, is enriched with a unique scientific combination+ of nutrients which have been scientifically researched and proven to help give your child a solid foundation to be mentally sharp and physically active.
New Junior Horlicks is easy-to-digest, and has a taste little children love.
3 STEPS TO A NOURISHING AND DELICIOUS DRINK
Take three heaped teaspoonfuls of Junior Horlicks (25g) in a cup.
Add a little hot (not boiling) milk and stir to make a paste.
Stirring briskly, slowly add hot or cold milk as desired. Add sugar to taste.
MALTED FOOD
(Proprietary Food)
MADE IN INDIA BY
SMITHKLINE BEECHAM
CONSUMER HEALTHCARE LTD.
NABHA-147 201.
Under licence from
HORLICKS LIMITED, U.K.
NET WT. 500g
BEST BEFORE WITHIN 12 MONTHS FROM THE DATE OF PACKAGING.
M.R.P.: Rs.
(Incl. of all taxes)
PKD. :
B.No. :
8 901571 000074

(3) Marketing muscles: By the beginning of the '80s *Horlicks* was a wonderful success story; it had already crossed the Rs. 100 crores mark. The only area where HMM had to be careful was the all-important one — the product. Since HMM did not have the necessary infrastructure to manufacture the product, a decision had to be taken as to how the product should be produced. After lengthy discussions, it was agreed that the best route would be through 'contract manufacturing', and fortunately, there were already established manufacturers of biscuits.

Two very important decisions were taken at the same time:

(1) To ensure that the biscuit was of the highest QUALITY, as well as per agreed standard, an HMM Quality Control Manager would be posted at the factory site of the contracted manufacturer. No batch of the manufactured goods could pass through the factory gates without his approval.
(2) Since freight would be an important element in the total cost structure, HMM should have at least one manufacturer in each region of North, South, East and West. For obvious reasons South and East received priority. In fact for the South (which contributed 60% to the *Horlicks* business), the search was for two manufacturers: one in Hyderabad and another in Tamilnadu (the single biggest state of *Horlicks* users).

Introduction and its Performance

Horlicks Biscuits were thus introduced in the South and the East in the early '90s. Within a short time it was evident that the product was a winner. During the first year of its operation, HMM notched up a sale of Rs. 2 crores. In 1998, the latest year for which information is available, the *Horlicks Biscuits* sale was Rs. 30 crores.

Excellent packaging and the strong equity of the parent brand *Horlicks*, along with a very strong distribution network have resulted in the phenomenal success of *Horlicks Biscuits*. It has shown superb growth performance and has been showing double digit growth in volume terms.

Table 7.1 *Volume Sales*

Region	Tons
South	3213
East	3077
West	433
North	257
Others	340
All India	7320

Horlicks Biscuits provide all the natural goodness of *Horlicks* and are the most nutritious biscuits in the market. The strategy of *Horlicks Biscuits* is to extend the *Horlicks* franchise to new usage occasions and gain business from the growing biscuit market by securing the parent product's nutritional supremacy and nourishment credibility.

Subsequent to this successful line extension, it was decided to further extend the *Horlicks* equity to the cream biscuits segment and *Horlicks Sandwich Biscuits* were launched in 1996. The biscuits were launched in three variants: Chocolate, Malt and Elaichi. Each 100gm pack was equal to 2 cups of *Horlicks* nourishment.

Further Brand Extensions

Horlicks' Other Brand Extensions

In recent years SmithKline Beecham have made further use of the Brand Equity of *Horlicks* by extending it to three other products:

(1) *Junior Horlicks*

The rationale behind this extension is to catch targetted consumers when they are young, so that as they grow, so does the brand. The nutritional value of the product has been further enhanced by adding ingredients suitable for children between the ages of 1 and 3. In a way parents would be instrumental in introducing the brand to the children, so that these children will be growing up on *Horlicks*.

NEW
SMART NUTRIENTS™
MOTHER'S
Horlicks
nourishing food drink
For pregnant and breast-feeding mothers

Healthy Mothers
for Healthy Babies
DIRECTIONS FOR USE
NEW
SMART NUTRIENTS™
MOTHER'S
Horlicks
nourishing food drink
For pregnant and breast-feeding mothers
NUTRITION FACTS
SMART NUTRIENTS™
CONTAINS ADDED FLAVOUR
MALTED FOOD
(Proprietary Food)
SMITHKLINE BEECHAM
CONSUMER HEALTHCARE LTD.
Under licence from
HORLICKS LIMITED, U.K.
NET WT. 500g
BEST BEFORE WITHIN 12 MONTHS
FROM THE DATE OF PACKAGING.
M.R.P.: Rs.
(Incl. of all taxes)
PKD. :
B.No. :
SB SmithKline Beecham

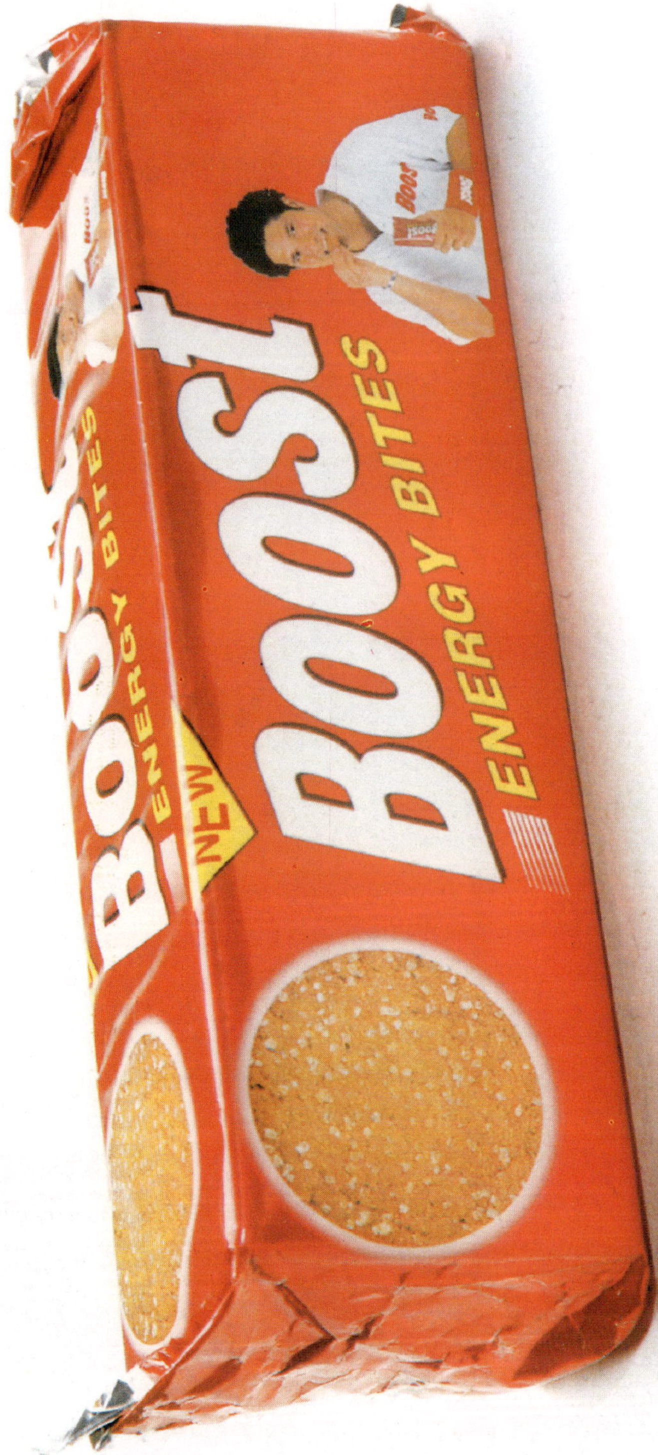
NEW
Boost
ENERGY BITES

Since introduction this extended brand has done well, and today its sale is approximately 10% of the mother brand *Horlicks*. For more reasons than one it would appear that the extension has been a wise one. As they say, 'Catch them young and keep them forever!'

(2) *Mother's Horlicks*

Once again the rationale for this extension is to some extent similar to that behind *Junior Horlicks* — mothers need special nourishment at special or specific times and this extended brand will give her that. Special nutritional ingredients necessary for mothers have been added to make this brand more suitable for her. The brand today has 30 per cent of the pregnancy supplement market.

This extended brand is a replacement of the earlier brand *Mother's Special*.

(3) *Chocolate Horlicks*

Originally this brand was introduced by adding chocolate flavour, mainly to compete with *Complan* chocolate brand, which is a good seller. Since the mother brand *Horlicks* is used with water, consumers of this brand also did the same, with unsatisfactory results. Since then the product has been reformulated so that the consumer can get a very satisfactory drink by preparing it with water.

Its sale is approximately 5 per cent of the overall *Horlicks* sales.

Boost Extension

Boost Biscuits

With the success of *Horlicks Biscuits*, SmithKline Beecham Consumer Healthcare decided to produce *Boost* biscuits. In one of the case studies, appearing in this book, I have discussed *Boost* — how it was successfully launched in mid-'75, and how it is now an important brand for HMM. Naturally the management decided to extend that brand also to the field of biscuits, i.e., *Boost Biscuits*. It was a natural marketing decision to fully exploit the brand's awareness and acceptance in the consumer's mind.

8

POWER OF BRANDING

Niche Marketing

GENTEEL

Sometime in the early '70s — I was then working as Marketing Director of Home Products Marketing Agency (a Sarabhai organisation) — I had gone to give some clothes (silk and woollen) for dry-cleaning. I was taken aback, not so much by the price the shop was charging, but by the pile of clothes a young lady gave for dry-cleaning. I thought it must cost her a fortune.

I went back home thinking that there had to be a better way, or rather an inexpensive way, to get your woollen and silk clothes washed. You see, at that time I was selling *Det* and *Sway*, and *Surf* was the brand leader. But none of these brands were really suitable for washing woollen and silk clothes. I recollected that when I was a boy, our house used to have *Lux Flakes*, which were used only for expensive silk and woollen clothes. Since then the product had dropped out of the market. I started thinking that if we could produce something like that, we may have a winner on our hands. Thus an idea was born, which finally translated into a concrete product, *Genteel*, the current brand leader in this segment.

But the whole process of formulating and introducing *Genteel* was not that simple. First, the idea needed to be accepted by R&D. At the next New Product Development Committee meeting, I asked the

genteel
LIQUID WASHING DETERGENT
25 YEARS OF TRUST
FREE GIFT
OFFE
THE SAFEST HOME WASH FOR DELICATE CLOTHE

WOOLMARK
APPROVED
WOOLMARK
PURE NEW WOOL
Ezee
FOR DELICATE AND EXPENSIVE CLOTHES

New Product Development Manager to put up a brief. To make sure that in principle R&D would agree to such a brief, Marketing interacted with them to make sure that not only did they understand what we had in mind, but that we also had the necessary technological expertise to create such a product.

During the meeting of the New Product Development Committee one thing became quite clear: there was no question of producing 'flakes', but in fact we would be better off with a liquid, rather than a powder. Marketing thought that instead of being a disqualifier, a detergent in liquid form could be turned into a distinct advantage — it would distinguish our product from the usual powder products like *Surf*, *Det* or *Sway*.

Next came the research project, mainly to find out:

(1) the acceptance of the proposition; and
(2) the size of such a market.

The findings were encouraging. We also discovered that, even at that time, some households were already using the current brands, *Surf* and *Det* for washing their woollen and silk clothes, particularly sweaters and sarees, etc. They welcomed the idea of having a better product specifically manufactured to wash their expensive silk and woollen clothes. In other words, we had a ready-made market waiting for a better product. However, there were doubts as to whether it would be safe to wash expensive garments at home, which at the moment went for dry-cleaning.

Marketing, therefore, realised that in our communication objective we had not only to educate the housewives about the proficiency of the product, but also assure them that their expensive clothes, whether silk or wool, would be safe while being washed at home, and that they need not go to the dry-cleaners any more. And of course, it would cost much, much less. We, therefore, had a difficult proposition in hand. How do you communicate so many messages in one ad? Remember, at that time TV advertising had not started yet, the main medium was the press. We had been trained that, to be successful, only one message should be delivered, so that consumers could easily remember it.

Brand Name

The next item on the agenda was the creation of a brand name. By definition the market would be a small one, at least initially (as compared to the total detergent market). Naturally the temptation was to tag on to either *Det* or *Sway*, and get the benefit of the 'Umbrella Brand' theory. I was against such a move. In fact, the Group Chairman, was very much in favour of tagging on to *Det*, which at that time enjoyed a somewhat better quality image. I was against such a move because of two important reasons:

(1) I wanted to give the product a new and special image, thereby offering it as a different and better product than all the detergent brands available at that time in India.

(2) Since *Surf* was the brand leader (approx. 75%) those currently using detergent powders for washing silk and woollen garments, would form the biggest chunk of current detergent brand users.

Fortunately, because the product was going to be in a liquid form, it would be easier to differentiate from the current detergent brands.

There was one other important consideration. I thought that if we had a different name, maybe through that name, we could solve part of the communication problem. Thus the brand name 'GENTEEL' was born. The advertising agency came up with the idea of producing a label which said:

'Genteel' — *gentle wash for your expensive clothes*
(like silk and woollen)

But when we went to register the brand name, we were told, that it could not be registered. The only way out was to introduce the brand, let it sell for nine months or so, and then get the whole label registered (since it had already been in use). Nobody would then be able to use the same brand name in the same style and logo. We accepted this revised suggestion, and went ahead with the brand name.

Along with the label design, we also decided to develop a special bottle, which would again be unique to the brand. In other words, the bottle, the label, the brand name, the logo, everything together would give the product a unique identity.

The rest is history.

Today, after 20 years, this brand is still the brand leader — almost generic. And although the company has been sold, and most of the other brands have, more or less, disappeared from the market, *Genteel* still continues to be the brand leader in this niche market.

Postscript

Today, unfortunately, Swastik Oil Mills are in new hands — the Sarabhais have sold it to one Mr. Shah. Therefore I cannot quote actual figures. However, to what extent the brand caught the imagination of the consumers, can best be illustrated by an incident which occurred at my residence in 1987.

Subsequent to leaving the Sarabhais in mid-'72, I also left Mumbai and settled down in New Delhi. After almost 15 years, one day I handed over my woollen sweater to our maid, to wash it at home in *Genteel*. To make sure that she used only *Genteel* (and not *Surf*), I asked her to not only confirm that we had *Genteel* at home, but to actually show me the bottle — she showed me a bottle of *Ezee* (manufactured by Godrej), which it appeared had filled up the vacuum, since *Genteel* was no longer regularly available in the market. As far as she was concerned, she was using *Genteel*, inspite of the fact that not only was the brand name different, the shapes of the two bottles were also different. Such is the strength of the brand. *Genteel* has become almost a generic name (like *Dalda* for all types of vanaspati).

A New Brand Idea — Niche Marketing

HAPPINESS

Background

In India, the housewife is totally convinced that milk is the prime source of nutrition. It is for this reason that Operation Flood has become such a big success. In some big cities like Delhi, an adequate supply of milk is assured through organisations, such as Mother Dairy, even though the quality and taste of this milk is not as good as that of Punjab and Haryana. But this does not hold good for all cities or states, where the milk is either of poor quality or in short supply.

Then mothers have a problem because their children are not very keen to drink this milk. But they believe that milk is the prime source of energy and nourishment and therefore, their children should drink it. Children, on the other hand, do not like to drink milk. How then is the mother going to ensure that the child drinks milk?

This was seen as an ideal opportunity to introduce a product that would entice a child into drinking milk happily. From a marketing man's point of view, a brilliant idea is born. Obviously, in this situation if the company could introduce a brand which would help mothers ensure that the child drinks milk happily, it would have a successful brand in the market.

Proposition and Brand Brief

There was, therefore, a market for a new range of flavours that children would like and which could be easily mixed with milk and, of course, would not cost too much.

The question raised by the Marketing Manager at this stage was: can we make a product which would offer unique and exciting flavours at a reasonable price? Since it must readily mix with cold or hot milk, it should be a free-flowing powder and to make sure that it does not cost much, a 400gm pack should provide at least 60 servings.

DELICIOUS MILK FLAVOURING
HAPPINESS
FRUIT CHOCOLATE

HAPPINESS

Now HAPPINESS gives milk a great new taste. Just a little HAPPINESS is all it takes to make milk a delightful drink for your child. See him smile through his milk-times. HAPPINESS is a blend of natural and wholesome ingredients that makes milk richer than ever.

HAPPINESS FRUIT CHOCOLATE is the exotic taste that's lightly flavoured with chocolate and a smacking of delicious fruit, to make milk different. Ingredients: Wheat, barley malt, malt extract, caramel and cocoa powder. Artificially flavoured.

Also available in Strawberry Twist flavour.

HAPPINESS

A little HAPPINESS goes a long way.
1. Stir in just 1 teaspoonful of HAPPINESS in a glass of hot or cold milk.
2. Add sugar to taste, and a delicious drink is ready.

Since you need to use so little, a bottle of HAPPINESS will last you a long, long time.

60 delicious servings!

Made in India by
**HMM LIMITED,
NABHA-147 201.**
under licence from
Beecham Group, p.l.c. U.K.
Net Weight: 400 g
Max. Price: Rs
(Local Taxes Extra)
Packed:

A brand brief was accordingly issued. The target audience are obviously urban households in the income group of Rs 500 and above (in 1980), with at least one child drinking milk. Although the final user would be the child, the decision maker would be either the child or the mother, but for obvious reasons the buyer would generally be the mother. The product must have a unique range of milk flavourings and at the same time should be concentrated so that it would be economical to use. The consumer's benefit was that the product would make milk-drinking a more enjoyable experience for children. Research was carried out on various conceptual appeals and it became apparent that children's enjoyment was the most acceptable concept for this brand.

Brand name

Research has also shown that in the past the success of a brand depended also on effective and appropriate naming. Further research was conducted from a shortlist of 6 names to find out which of these names appeared to be most appropriate for the brand. 'Happiness' emerged as the winner. The name naturally carried the right message to the mothers to whom it signified what the product was purported to do, namely, make children drink milk happily. As a part of the description for the product Marketing added the words "Delicious Milk Flavouring".

Now came the question of flavours. Marketing had to bear in mind two important factors: firstly, it must match possible consumer expectations; and secondly, it must be unique. Marketing came out with two flavours — Fruit Chocolate and Strawberry Twist. These are not straightforward chocolate and strawberry flavours, but variations of chocolate with toppings of some other flavour, blended with strawberry. The advantages of mixed flavours are that it is a unique experience, and from the company's point of view, no one can easily imitate these flavours.

Packaging

Marketing selected a glass jar because it was possible to give a unique shape to the jar. It was also possible to give it a wide mouthed look which was also elegant to look at. Marketing also knew that after-use of a container is a very important consideration for the Indian housewife.

Label and logo design

For obvious reasons, the label must reflect the aura of the brand name. It must also give the ingredient story, talk particularly of the unique flavour range and definitely address the issue of economy. In other words, with the brand name, logo and label, the brand must create a distinctive feel, so that over a period it develops a distinct personality of its own.

The company's advertising agents, Hindustan Thompson Associates, were briefed accordingly. They came up with various suggestions. After a number of suggestions were discussed with the marketing team, they finally created a label, which not only had a human element, but also specifically gave information on the flavour. Also, the brand name could be read easily from a distance, which is important in India where there are quite a lot of rather small outlets, with dark interiors.

Pricing

This, of course, was a very important factor in the total overall marketing of a brand. Since Marketing knew that the product was meant for children in homes with an income of Rs. 500 plus, the pricing of the product assumed even greater significance. Research results showed that Rs. 16/- per bottle of 400gm, which gives 60 servings, would be considered a reasonable price by housewives.

Marketing communication

Then came the most important aspect and that was how to make the brand known. Once again, in close co-operation with their advertising agents, Hindustan Thompson Associates, a communication strategy was developed. The communication objectives were to convey the ethos of enjoyment, to promote the unique flavour range, and of course, to promote the theme of economy.

After several presentations and interactions with the marketing team, this is what marketing eventually selected. Marketing felt that not only did it give a story, but the headline was a show-stopper. It was felt that any mother looking at that advertisement would immediately stop and try to find out what the brand was talking about. Since TV and cinema are very important media for communication, an appropriate audio-visual story was also developed.

The story went something like this. It showed a split second screen with two boys playing with building blocks. The one on the left hand side has milk without any *Happiness* added, whereas the one on the right has a glass of milk with *Happiness* added. The boy on the left does not want to drink plain milk. He quickly exchanges his glass for the one which has *Happiness* added. The other boy, when he finds that his glass has no *Happiness*, does not complain about the exchange but quickly adds *Happiness* to his glass of milk. Both of them are then happy to drink their milk.

Yes! *Happiness* is saying yes to milk!

Final go ahead

Marketing then did a final research (which can be called the final process of quality control), of the total package, i.e., the product, packaging, brand name, price, as well as communication strategy. The research objectives were to determine the overall expectations of the brand in its final form; to check whether the advertising was impressionable, relevant and creditable, as well as to check whether the same held true for the pack as well.

The main findings were very encouraging indeed. Marketing thought that the overall performance of the brand on attributes of communication and packaging were good. It was also found that the unique flavours of the brand were well-liked. The children not only liked the taste, it further became a children's favourite. As far as communication was concerned, 85 per cent of the mothers were interested enough to look for the brand after reading the advertisement. Similarly, 82 per cent of the mothers expressed their willingness to try the product.

There was evidence that after trying the product there was further likelihood that some of them would become regular users. 85 per cent were motivated by the advertising to look for further information. The mothers felt that the advertisement itself highlighted the problem they regularly faced with their children, as far as drinking of milk was concerned. Definite empathy was created by the ad. Everybody liked the children shown in the advertisement and could definitely relate to the children.

The label did communicate the health value of the product as well as the economy of the brand. In other words, the product lived up to the brand brief. The product had a range of milk flavouring which was unique. It also made milk a more enjoyable experience for children and, therefore, the brand itself satisfied the need for which the idea had been visualised—when marketing had originally decided to capitalise on the opportunity arising out of Operation Flood.

Performance

During the first six months, the brand did very well; there was a steady increase in sales as the company kept on extending distribution. The next three months saw the stabilisation of sales, and then suddenly sales seemed to plummet. The Marketing Manager pushed the panic button and a quick tracking research was initiated. The results gave a clear insight into what was happening — very few repeat purchases were being made. Once the novelty of the product wore out, housewives were just not coming back for the second or the third bottle.

Conclusion

What actually happened is that what Marketing thought of as a very good 'Niche Marketing' strategy, was not actually a very bright idea! Mothers were looking for an underpinning of health benefit, over and above mere taste acceptance. But these benefits were already being catered for by the existing brands — *Bournvita, Boost, Maltova,* etc., in the brown powder segment.

Upgrading in a New Environment

SUPER 777 BAR

It was Nov./Dec., 1971. I was on a market visit in the Kolhapur/Sholapur area of Maharashtra, with my Regional Sales Manager. Tata's *501 Bar Soap* was by far the leader in the laundry soap segment. In fact there were no other brands except *777 Bar* (Swastik's), worth the name in that segment, and the main competition came from the unorganized sector. Lever had also introduced their detergent cake *Rin*; followed by *Det* which was introduced a few months later, by our company Swastik (Sarabhai).

I noticed that in smaller towns like Kolhapur/Sholapur, demand for the 'cake', and of course the bar soap far outweighed the demand for 'powder'. This was understandable since in these small towns clothes were washed by the river banks or near the village (or town) well. Water from taps, not being easily available, precluded the use of buckets. In other words, I could clearly see good potential, for quite some time to come, for bar/cake soap detergent. I noticed another phenomenon during this market visit. Although *Tata 501 Bar* was a footlong bar, many of the customers generally bought only a part of it, the shopkeeper cutting a small portion (usually 2 or 3 inches long), thus dividing the bar into six such portions. Inquiries revealed that very rarely was the *501 Bar* sold in its entirety to a consumer. In fact the bar had serrations, every 2 inches, to facilitate such cutting.

Swastik also had a bar soap — *777 Bar*, but it was a poor second. Inquiries revealed that past attempts to increase market share to the same level of the *501 Bar*, had met with only limited success. Since by then I knew that the washing powder performance for detergent is superior to that of soap, I thought maybe we should think of entering this market with a detergent bar. An idea came to mind now which ultimately led to the introduction of the 'Super 777 Bar'.

Before we go into details, as to how the product was developed, let's look at the washing products market of that time.

SUPER 777
detergent washing bar

**PAISA BACHAO
SAFEDI BADHAO**

Profile of the Washing Products Market

The consumer offtake of washing materials in 1972 was 3,98,975 tons, of which 11.9 per cent was detergent solids and powders, and the remaining 88.1 per cent supplied by soap cakes and bars. Of the cakes and bars market, detergent cakes and bars constituted 12 per cent of the market, soap cakes/bars had a share of 88 per cent.

However, 1973 witnessed a growth rate of 45 per cent as compared to 1972 in the detergent solids market, i.e., detergent solids was the growth market of the future.

Detergent solids market

Detergent solids were divided into 2 categories — Popular and Premium. The distinction in the detergent solids market is based on the price per kg of the material. If 1kg of a detergent costs Rs. 15/- and above, it is a Premium detergent. If it is below Rs. 15/-, it is classified as a Popular detergent. ORG has laid down this definition of the Premium and Popular segments. The percentage share of the detergent in the total washing materials market has been steadily increasing. In 1972, detergents had 12% of the market; by the end of 1975 the market share had grown to 15.5 per cent.

In the Premium category, during Phase 1, i.e., 1972-1975 there were 2 major brands in the detergent solids group — *Rin* and *Det*; and 2 brands in the detergent powders group — *Surf* and *Det*. In the Popular market, there was Tata's *Bonus* (detergent cake), which had a 28% market share of the detergent solids market. The Premium detergents during this period had an active market share around 16% and the Popular around 12%. This was adequate when compared to the soaps which had a very large market share (around 80%).

Prices

During Phase 1, i.e., 1972-1975, premium detergent cakes like *Rin* and *Det* were selling at around Re. 0.90 per cake of 135gm. *Super 777* of the popular category was selling at Re. 0.90 per bar of

180gm. By 1974, the price had risen to Re. 1.22 for *Rin* and *Det* and Re. 1.00 for *Super 777*.

The premium brands advertised, to highlight cleaning power and whiteness, whereas the popular brands emphasised the aspect of economy in their advertising. The major share of offtake for the premium brands came from the Metros and Class 1 towns.

Brand shares

Table 8.1 *Brand Shares — All India (Jan.-Dec.)*

	1972 Tons	% Share
PREMIUM		
Rin	7820	54.8
Det	2282	16.0
POPULAR		
Bonus	4084	28.6
Super 777	—	—

Detergent Bar

But, converting the original idea that we had discussed earlier into a product, was not easy. First, by definition, if we wanted a footlong bar of detergent the cost would be prohibitive, so we were told by R&D. The way out, again R&D suggested, was to add buffer, so as to not only reduce cost, but also give the required size impression.

Once we perfected the 'mixture', after quite a few trials, the next problem was how to cut the bar into 6 small portions, since a detergent bar would be that much harder to cut. Again, R&D found a way out, instead of making a footlong bar, the size was reduced to half, i.e., 6 inches long. R&D provided serration in such a way (deeper), that the shopkeeper would need very little effort to cut it into smaller portions. In other words, a way was found to sell to the consumer, in exactly the same way as he was accustomed to buying, but a more efficient product (at more or less the same price). Communication thus became much more simple — 'more washing power'. And the fact that it was a 'detergent' bar, provided the reason why. Thus was born *Super 777* bar.

Introduction to *Super 777*

India experienced an acute shortage of vegetable oils in 1972. Swastik, complying with the Government policies (discounting edible oils for manufacture of soaps), decided to introduce a detergent bar with the brand name, *Super 777* (in place of *777 Bar Soap*).

Super 777 bar was introduced in December 1972. *Super 777* was positioned to compete with the existing oil-based bar soaps by offering the consumer a superior product at an economical price. The idea behind this product did not make the consumer change his washing habits, (but offered him a product at an economical price). At the time of introducing *Super 777*, *777 Bar Soap* was fairly well-established in the washing materials market and the name association was maintained, so as to encash the awareness already created. The objective was not to suggest something radically different from the material presently being used by the consumer but to offer an improved version of the same. Bar soaps having the largest market share, were being sold in small pieces, all over the semi-urban and rural markets. The idea was to introduce a product very similar in appearance to soaps, but with better washing and cleaning properties. We decided to have cuts on the bar so that it could be broken and sold in smaller units. Further, this product was meant to cater to the lower and middle income groups whose washing habits included only soaps.

Super 777 was positioned to fill the slot between premium detergent solids at one end and soap cakes and bars at the other. Premium detergent brands were too high-priced, and soap cakes and bars did not give optimum washing efficiency though they were cheaper. *Super 777* attempted to combine the washing efficiency of a detergent with the price economy of the washing soaps. This segment was classified as the popular detergent solids segment. This required educating the consumers to accept the concept of a 'detergent'. The target audience for this brand being semi-literate, the communication had to be kept simple, with a combination of audio and visual, to explain the product concept.

What *Super 777* Offered to its Consumers

It was a specially formulated 'Detergent' bar very effective in both hard and soft water. The product contained the following —

(a) Active Detergent - to remove dirt thoroughly and quickly.
    Matter (12%)   - to tie up water hardness.
                      - to hold back dirt in the water so as to prevent redeposition prior to rinsing.
                      - the ability to retain the same cleaning power in both hard and soft water.
(b) Sequestering   - to reduce water hardness.
                      - to prevent redeposition of dirt.
                      - to emulsify oily and greasy dirt.
(c) Optical Whitener - to bring about a visual whitening effect by the concept of "fluorescence", i.e., by reflecting ultraviolet rays.

The product

The bar had 4 cuts and was yellow in colour. This was done because it should look similar to bar soap (say *501*, etc.)

Weight : 180gm

Colour : Yellow

Appearance : Similar to a bar soap with 4 cuts. The bar can be broken into pieces at these cuts. The names Swastik and *Super 777* were stamped on both sides in English, on each cut.

Consumer profile

Sex   : Both Female and Male
Age   : 15+
Education : Illiterate   - 25%
            Below S.S.C.   - 30%
            S.S.C./Undergrad.   - 30%
            Graduate and above   - 15%

Income : Lower middle - Rs. 200-500 pm
        Middle   - Rs. 500-750 pm

Price

The retail price of *Super Bar* varied from 90 to 95 paise in the markets.

Advertising and promotion

The advertising objectives of *Super 777* were to introduce to the consumer the concept of a quality detergent bar which had definite advantages over soaps. The ads also highlighted the price advantage. The USP of *Super 777* was: "For a whiter wash at a lower cost"; "Paise bachao, Safedi badao". The communication platform sought to focus on the innovation and to emphasise the economy, whiteness and cleaning power, as well as to re-emphasise economy *vis-à-vis* bar soaps.

Packaging

The bar was wrapped in an attractive yellow and red wrapper. The brand name was printed on the bar in both Hindi and English. There were 60 bars to a cardboard box.

The response to the product was due to the following factors:

(1) The advertising gave the product a lot of quick trials and promised the consumer a lot of advantages.
(2) The product did meet the promises it had made in the ad.
(3) Users of *Super 777* were very much satisfied with the product; brand loyalty, which is the key to developing brand equity, started increasing.

Consumer offtake

The total market for detergent cakes and bars were 14266 tons in 1973 and witnessed a growth of 39.4%. In 1974 there was a growth of 36.4%. The total offtake for *Super 777* (urban and rural) in 1973 was 1242 tons with a market share of 6.2%. In 1974 consumer offtake was 6153 tons with a market share of 22.7%. In 1975 market share was 28.1% with a total offtake of 8693 tons.

Finally in 1977 the total offtake reached 16972 tons. It was indeed a success story!

Product positioning

Super Bar was placed against the bar soap and the soap cake markets in the organized segment. To carve for itself a substantial share in the market, campaign efforts were designed to appeal to the middle and lower income categories in the metros and Class 1 cities, and to all income groups in Classes 3, 4 and rural markets.

Launch

The product was launched in the Western region in November 1972. By March 1973 it was launched in the Southern region. In the East and the North it was launched by October 1973. The product received very good response immediately and the consumers accepted it as a new concept detergent washing bar.

Sales

The product gained very good response almost immediately. The sales in 1972 was 142 tons. Sales shot up to 5904 tons in '73-'74. Sales increased steadily and by 1977 it reached 16972 tons.

9

ENHANCING BRAND IMAGE THROUGH PROMOTIONS

The use of sales promotion, throughout the world, has most often been to 'buy' short term extra sales. India is no exception. Its role has usually been 'tactical' — the solving of immediate problems, like a fall in sales, or a declining trend (which therefore needs a shot in the arm) — rather than the building of a brand's long term strength.

In the next few pages I will be talking about two successful examples of sales promotion which have contributed to building added value to the brand, and thus helped in building Brand Equity. It is a pity that more often than not, sales promotion is used mainly to get temporary benefits, i.e., an increase in sales at that point of time.

The first of the two case studies is known as the '*Boost* Train Picture Cards' promotion; and the second the *Bournvita Book of Knowledge* promotion — both the products are in the same category, namely the brown powder sector of the Malted Milkfood market. Both brands, designed for consumption by children, but purchased by their mothers, have a twin focus for their loyalty-building activities: child appeal and mother approval.

Cadbury's Bournvita

BOOK OF KNOWLEDGE

BOURNVITA Book of Knowledge

Background

During the 1970s Bournvita's advertising claim, 'Brought up Right–*Bournvita* Bright', was supported by a very popular radio programme, 'The *Bournvita* Quiz Contest'. This was an inter-school quiz involving participation from schools in Mumbai, Delhi, Calcutta and Chennai. It was broadcast from seven stations — Mumbai, Pune, Nagpur, Calcutta, Delhi, Chennai, Trichy — and created a lot of audience interest and involvement, particularly among children and other members of the family.

Objective

To enhance the brand image of *Bournvita* by supporting the main advertising proposition of the brand: 'Brought up Right–*Bournvita* Bright', thus building an enduring consumer group for the brand.

The promotion

Consumers sending in two proofs of purchase from any size of *Bournvita* were offered FREE the *Bournvita Book of Knowledge*, a compendium of questions and answers from the *Bournvita* Quiz Contest for the year 1972-73.

Results

Demand for the *Bournvita Book of Knowledge* was so great that a substantial reprint was required. Market research indicated very high recall and a linkage in the public's mind between *Bournvita*, the Quiz Contest and the *Book of Knowledge*, ranging from 49% in Delhi to 66% in Madras.

The scheme was therefore continued in subsequent years, with further annual compendiums of questions and answers, slight modifications being made to these later volumes of the *Bournvita Book of Knowledge* in the light of experience. Over a quarter of a million books have been sent out over the years.

Bournvita's brand share increased by 3 percentage points in each of the first years of this promotional programme. Scores for the number of consumers buying only *Bournvita* and no other competitive brand solidified to 46% in Calcutta, and went as high as 68% in Delhi.

Comment

This is a first class example of sales promotion being used successfully in a *strategic* role. 'Strategic' as opposed to 'tactical' in the sense that the programme ran over a lengthy period of time, several years. It was not just a quick in-and-out tactical operation designed to solve a particular problem or exploit a specific opportunity that had arisen in the short term. 'Strategic' too in that the *Book of Knowledge* was integrally related to the *Bournvita* Quiz Contest and in turn to the advertising proposition: 'Brought up Right–*Bournvita* Bright'.

The promotional programme thus supported the central thrust of the brand's marketing strategy. It took the fleeting words of the radio programmes and bestowed upon them a physical, tangible, permanent dimension in the form of the Book. It continued to communicate the brand proposition to consumers in their homes in between broadcasts of the Quiz Contest. It linked this popular programme firmly to the purchase of *Bournvita* by requiring two proofs of purchase to obtain the Book.

The Boost Train Album

BOOST Train Picture Cards

Background

Boost, a malt chocolate milk drink, was launched in 1976 as HMM's entry into the brown powder sector (HMM's brand *Horlicks* having already established its leading position in the white powder sector). After successfully test marketing it in Kerala the brand had reached national distribution by 1980. Sales continued to grow until 1982, but seemed then to have reached a plateau.

A wide-ranging review of the brand and its competition nonetheless indicated that the positioning of *Boost* as an energy drink for children was correct. In-depth qualitative research confirmed the strength of the advertising which had used the theme of trains to communicate the proposition: '*Boost*: the energy fuel for an active life. Taken regularly it helps to improve both physical and mental energy'. The need was for this proposition to be marketed with renewed vigour, in a rejuvenated form. HMM decided to turn to sales promotion to provide this fresh thrust.

Objective

To enhance brand equity by supporting theme advertising, and thereby increasing brand loyalty which would automatically result in increased sales.

The promotion

One of a series of 12 coloured picture cards was packed FREE in every 500gm pack of *Boost* (the larger of two sizes) throughout the six month promotional period. These picture cards illustrated famous trains from the history of railways around the world. The cards were contained in polythene pouches, 10 cm × 6.7 cm, sealed on all sides.

Four different picture cards were made available in packs in each of the first three months of the promotion, and the process was repeated in the second three months to give the consumer a further opportunity to collect all 12 cards. All 500gm packs were flashed on the front with an announcement of the promotion, referring the consumer for full details to the back of the label in the case of the 500gm jar, and to the back of the pack in the case of the 500gm refill pack.

Each picture card had a tear-off strip on its right hand side, printed with a number from 1 to 12. Sending in two of these strips qualified the consumer to receive, FREE, an album with spaces in which to paste the picture cards. The album contained much additional background information on, for example, the early history of trains; the expansion of railways round the world; the beginnings of underground railways; the advent of diesel and electric traction; the development of commuter services; great railwaymen; railways in India; unusual facts; glossary of railway terms; the future of trains, etc.

The album also contained a page with spaces for 6 further tear-off strips from the picture cards to be pasted down. No duplicates were allowed — the strips had to carry 6 different numbers from six different cards (these numbers corresponding to the numbered spaces allocated in the album to the picture cards themselves). The first 100 consumers to mail in this page containing the six strips would win a prize of an expensive electric train set.

Advertisements announcing and describing this promotion replaced the usual *Boost* 'theme' advertisements during August-November 1984. A special TV video film was created for this promotion. During the first month point-of-purchase display materials announced the promotion and highlighted the picture cards. During the second month new display materials highlighted the album. In the fourth month yet new display materials highlighted the album, as well as the electric train set.

This promotion marked the first co-operation between The Sales Machine in London, an international sales promotion agency, and HMM Ltd.

Results

Against a target increase in sales of 12.5 per cent during the six month promotional period, sales increased by 16.6 per cent. Against an estimate of 22,000 applications for the album, 61,147 were applied for. This represented almost exactly 10% of the 500gm packs sold during the six months being redeemed for albums. Almost one quarter of households buying *Boost* obtained an album. 4,020 entries were received for the electric train set. As a goodwill gesture HMM increased the number of train sets awarded from 100 to 300.

Both trade and consumer feedback on the promotion was extremely positive. Many children, as well as parents, wrote in expressing their appreciation of the offer. Market research conducted at the end of the promotion reported that it was regarded very favourably by mothers, who liked its educational aspect. It was the type of promotion they encouraged their children to participate in.

Comment

Picture cards inserted FREE in a pack is a classic collection technique when children are the consumers but their mothers are the purchasers. By giving the picture cards an educational character the mother is encouraged to pass them on to her child, and in turn the child encourages the mother to make further purchases of the brand offering the picture cards — rather than a competitive brand — in order to obtain further cards in the series.

The number of different picture cards in the series should not be greater than it is reasonable for a child to collect from his mother's purchases during the period of the promotion, though allowance can be made for the swapping of duplicate cards among school friends. An activity which can give additional word of mouth currency to the promotion: some children seeing their friends showing off and swapping these treasured cards return home and ask their mothers to buy *Boost* next time, instead of her normal brand. They want to be in on this new collection craze too! An album in which to insert the picture cards is a great stimulus to collection. As soon as the first card is stuck down, the remaining spaces look very blank indeed — they cry out to be filled! *Boost* was therefore right in making the album readily available, FREE, in return for only 2 proofs of purchase.

The high rate of participation at all levels of the promotion proved the appeal of trains as a subject, in the various ways it was treated in both the picture cards and the album. Best of all the train theme continued and extended the message of *Boost*'s advertising campaign. This new method of sales promotion was not an abandoning of all the careful marketing effort that had been put behind the brand previously, it was simply a new and impactive expression and execution of all that *Boost* had been saying about itself since its launch.

10

PROTECTION OF YOUR BRAND IN A COMPETITIVE ENVIRONMENT

HORLICKS vs. NESTOMALT

"Kill the competitor." That generally is the battle cry in the corporate world. Of course it is easier said than done. Yet, there are means and tactics, which, if properly executed, can make your competitor's life unbearable. I can recollect one such incident when I was working with HMM (now SmithKline Beecham Consumer Healthcare).

Background

I am talking about the time when *Horlicks* was by far the main product of HMM, whose sale contributed towards 80 per cent of the business, and 90 per cent of the profit. In the early '80s we learnt that Nestlé had decided to launch their product *Nestomalt* (which is a competitor to *Horlicks*) in India shortly. The brand was well-known throughout the world, particularly in the Far East. In fact in these markets *Nestomalt* had a better market share than *Horlicks*, in some markets quite substantially.

In India, on the other hand, *Horlicks* had a near monopoly position (*Viva* having a small share) in what is known as the 'white powder' market. We in HMM knew that Nestlé's product was good, and of course they were a successful company, with very good distribution channels.

HMM's Strategy Plan

Immediately upon receiving information about *Nestomalt*'s impending entry into the Indian market an emergency meeting of the Marketing Committee was called. The Managing Director of the company, who is normally not a member of the committee, attended the meeting, given the importance of the subject matter. After a prolonged discussion, the following decisions were taken:

(1) A special task force was created from the field force and placed under the leadership of General Manager Sales with 3 other members consisting of Regional Sales Managers of North, South and East. North, because Nestlé's headquarters is in Delhi, and therefore he was asked to keep a tab on Nestlé's activities in headquarters, through his counterpart in Delhi. South and East were *Horlicks'* strongholds, contributing approximately 90% of the *Horlicks* business. It was felt that Nestlé would probably introduce their brand first, either in the South or in the East.

   The task force's main agenda was to gather market intelligence, and to keep HQ informed about Nestlé's next move.

(2) It was agreed that with Nestlé's muscle and distribution network there was no question of stopping distribution of *Nestomalt*, but certainly HMM could make life difficult for Nestlé's salesmen, by taking suitable pre-emptive actions, just before the brand was to be introduced. It was therefore vital that HMM have precise information regarding the date of launch of their brand.

(3) Massive field activities needed to be planned which could be put into action at a day's notice, a week before *Nestomalt*'s entry date into the market.

(4) Similarly, advertising and promotional activities needed to be intensified, again to start a week in advance of *Nestomalt*'s entry into the market, and to be continued non-stop at least for the next three months. Emergency plans needed to be worked out so as to continue such activities, if required, for another 3 to 6 months.

The main reason behind this warlike campaign was to make Nestlé realize that getting a foothold within India for *Nestomalt* would not be easy — they would have to fight every inch of the way. HMM's argument went somewhat like this: *Nestomalt* was never going to be their main business, that position was held by *Nescafé* (they had not introduced chocolate then) and their baby food. Naturally if they are required to spend by far more than proportionate resources to obtain a small share of the market, Nestlé may think twice before pushing the brand for long. On the other hand, *Horlicks* was not only bread and butter, but also jam for HMM. Naturally HMM would put all they had behind this brand so that *Horlicks* would continue to have a dominant position in the white powder market.

To achieve the above, the major thrust would be largely through 'below the line' promotional activities. These activities included:

(1) Dealer promotions and special efforts in the field to increase STRs and display and merchandising.
(2) Consumer promotions to retain the loyalty of *Horlicks* consumers. These included:
    * Price-off on the 450gm pack. It was proposed to offer Rs. 2/- off on the consumer price of the 450gm pack.
    * Offer the 1kg pack at the price of the 800gm pack, thereby giving the consumer a saving of over Rs. 7.50.
    * Consumer contest offering very attractive prizes.
(3) Beefing-up of media inputs to the required level during the first three months of launch.

At the end of 6 months, a second consumer promotion would be mounted to regain consumers who may have shifted to *Nestomalt*.

Trade Deal

(1) The plan was to mount a trade deal during the first 15 days of *Nestomalt*'s launch. The trade deal would be mounted the day it was learnt that Nestlé had approached retailers with *Nestomalt* stocks.
(2) The trade deal would offer a 4.166%, that is, one free on twenty four, discount. This discount rate would be applicable for each pack size of *Horlicks* separately. Retailers who buy less than case

lots will also get the discount on their purchases at the rate of one free on twenty four.
(3) It was planned that a 45-days stock input would be made during the period the trade deal was in effect.
(4) The trade deal would cover all pack sizes of *Horlicks*. However in Chennai and Calcutta where the 1kg pack was being offered to consumers at the price of the 800gm pack, the trade deal would cover only the 450gm and 1kg packs.
(5) The wholesalers would get free stocks along with the invoices. The stock held by the wholesaler on the day the trade deal was launched would not be covered. However, they could utilize these stocks initially for the trade deal, but it would be ensured that at the end of the trade deal, the wholesalers would have the same quantity of stocks that they had held on the day the trade deal was launched.

Display Contest

(1) A display contest would be mounted for a period of 6 weeks in Chennai, Calcutta and the major towns of Kerala, the rest of Tamilnadu and the rest of West Bengal. Dealers would be briefed on the display contest along with selling-in of trade deal stocks.
(2) To enter the display contest dealers would have to make a qualifying purchase. The display contest would be judged on the basis of:

	Points
Quality of display	40
Location of display	25
Duration of display	20
Creativity/Impact of display	15
Total	100

(3) To ensure wide dealer participation in the display contest, all dealers who scored a minimum of 50 points in the display contest, would be entitled to a consolation prize. While briefing the dealer on the display contest, it was ensured that the dealer is made aware of the type of display that would win at least a consolation prize.

(4) It would be ensured that each participating dealer was visited twice for judging his display during the display contest. The dealer's signature would be taken on each visit as confirmation of visit.

(5) To achieve HMM's goal, and to enable marketing to execute the above mentioned plan, marketing needed extra marketing budget. The committee recommended that an amount equal to the yearly budget should be allocated only for this purpose, to be spent in the next 6 to 9 months, after the introduction of *Nestomalt*. The marketing team was able to convince the management of the need for this extra budget. The presence of the Managing Director during the meeting also helped.

Execution of the Plan

(1) Field activities

One of the main stockists of HMM, East, was also an important stockist of Nestlé. Regional Manager, East was able to lay his hands on the Introduction Plan of *Nestomalt* through this stockist about 10 days before D-Day.

On receipt of these details in HO immediate actions were taken to execute our plan one week before their launch date. The Marketing Director himself flew to Calcutta to supervise field activities in that region. General Manager, Sales, was asked to go to Chennai, to do similar supervision in the South. This was done since the document circulated by Nestlé stated that there would be simultaneous introduction in the East and the South. It was also agreed that at the end of each day Marketing Director and General Manager would exchange notes on the phone, so that both would be aware of what HMM was doing, and also whether any counter measures were being planned by Nestlé. Calcutta and Chennai were the main targets of HMM's activities, since by far these were the two main areas of *Horlicks* business. Not only were all dealers more than fully stocked, liberal usage of POP materials made these markets look as if the 'festive season' had arrived.

By the time Nestlé salesmen went into the market to introduce *Nestomalt*, they found very little space to display *Nestomalt* on the dealer's shelves. Of course, they could not do a good job of display of the brand, as well as of their POP materials. We all know how important it is for a new product to be seen through good display, and how important it is to use plenty of POP material at the time of introduction to draw the attention of potential customers. It is not for nothing that proper display of the brand and its POP material is called the 'silent salesman'.

Both the marketing Director and the General Manager Sales stayed on for a week to supervise any counter measures that needed to be taken immediately after the introduction of *Nestomalt*. Naturally they kept in constant touch with each other during that period.

(2) Advertising and promotional activities

Just three days before the introduction date of *Nestomalt*, a massive advertising campaign of *Horlicks* appeared in all the media available at that time in the South and East. It was a veritable blitzkrieg. You could not read a newspaper or a magazine without noticing the *Horlicks* ad. Same was the case with cinema (TV was not commercial at that time). Radio spots were used extensively, particularly in smaller towns.

Result

Obviously Nestlé was able to distribute *Nestomalt* fairly well in all the important markets, and also did a reasonable job of displaying the product and the POP materials, thanks to their strength in the market place.

At the end of a year, *Nestomalt* was able to obtain approximately 5% of the market share; but at what cost? They also realised that in time they might be able to increase that market share to 7, 8 or even 10%, but to achieve that they would have to commit a very high proportion of their resources. Alternatively if they utilized that part of their resources for their stronger brands like *Nescafé*, the reward would be proportionately much higher.

With reluctance, therefore, Nestlé decided, after about a year and a half, to gradually withdraw *Nestomalt* from the Indian market.

Conclusion

As HMM had planned meticulously, well in advance, as to how they were going to fight the battle, and then had executed the same in fine detail, HMM made *Nestomalt's* life very difficult indeed. On the other hand, Nestlé evidently came to the conclusion that it was better to lose this battle, but survive and win the war. They gathered together their remaining forces and continue as a successful company, by concentrating on their many other powerful brands.

11

BRAND MANAGEMENT

Customer is the King: Will Always Be

LIPTON'S YELLOW LABEL
vs.
BROOKE BOND'S RED LABEL

This happened in the early '60s when I was working for Lipton. Although Lipton Ltd., (at that time a subsidiary of the London company), was a successful tea company, unfortunately there was very little of what could be called 'marketing' activities, as distinct from sales activities.

As far as sales was concerned, the company had a well thought out sales organisation. The country was divided into six sales branches — one each at Calcutta, Delhi, Mumbai, Ahmedabad, Nagpur and Chennai. Each branch had a sales force of anything between 300 to 400 salesmen, with Sales Supervisors, Territory Managers, etc. All told we had approximately 2000 salesmen on an all-India basis. Each salesman was in-charge of a depot, to which the company sent stocks at regular intervals, and he did direct sales with ready stocks.

I am giving this background, so as to emphasise the fact that as far as marketing was concerned, it was all sales activities. We did have an Advertising Manager, but his function was really to produce POP materials, like posters, danglers, etc. All were sales oriented staff.

NEW
BRIGHT & RICH
LIPTON LONDON
Lipton
YELLOW LABEL
FINEST TEA BLEND
Premium Quality
FREE
an attractive mug with this pack
Lipton
YELLOW LABEL TEA
CTC
SPECIALLY SELECTED
Offer open in select cities till stocks last.
Normal pack also available.
Net Weight 500 g

NEW
EST. 1869
Brooke Bond
Red
Label
Tea
Now with Assam Super Tasters

The company did very little advertising. I can't recollect a single marketing or consumer research project undertaken during my 12-year term with them.

Background

As Assistant Manager of the Delhi branch, I needed to tour and visit the markets anything between 10 to 12 days a month. Looking back, I now realize that I owed a lot to these visits. They helped me understand the Indian market; but even more importantly I understood the need for such regular visits, if one wanted to be a successful marketing man.

During my visits to Punjab (Haryana was not born then) I noticed that particularly in the dhabas and roadside tea shops, the shop owners overwhelmingly preferred Brooke Bond's *Red Label* to Lipton's *Yellow Label*. We knew that both were Assam teas, and that these gave strong liquors. When I discussed the matter with some of these tea shop owners, invariably the answer was: "But Brooke Bond's *Red Label* gives stronger liquor". Some of them even went further, and said, "You improve your *Yellow Label* to give stronger liquor, and we shall use your brand also".

When I returned from one of these tours, I started thinking, that maybe there was something in what the tea shop keepers told me. If it was true that the people of Punjab preferred stronger liquor, that must be the reason why Brooke Bond's *Red Label* sale was so much more than Lipton's *Yellow Label*.

As I said earlier, there was no question of conducting market research. In fact, if I remember correctly there was no ORG or any other Marketing Research Company at that time. It was through market visits, talking to the dealers, and to the tea shop owners, for products like tea or coffee, that we could gather some information about consumer preferences. I therefore decided to include a paragraph in my report suggesting that the 'tea-testing' department at HO should look into this problem, and if possible send us 'improved' *Yellow Label* to find out its acceptance in those tea shops.

I did not realise at that time that I had stirred a hornet's nest. I had in fact questioned the ability of the company's 'tea-testing' department. How could they give us a better blend — *Yellow Label* was the best blend in that category of Assam tea! They came right back at me and re-confirmed that the leaf Brooke Bond used for their *Red Label* was much smaller, and frankly of inferior quality. To them Lipton's *Yellow Label* was by far the best quality in that category. That was that!

I discussed the matter further with my Branch Manager. He promised to check the position *vis-à-vis* my report, the next time he toured Punjab. This he did in a couple of months. Fortunately for me the feedback from the tea shops confirmed my observations. I therefore requested him to mention the same in his report also. I have to say that, inspite of HO's comments, as stated earlier, he supported my prognosis, and requested for a revised sample (blended to give stronger liquor) for testing at a few tea shops.

What we had not reckoned with, was the 'pride and prestige' of the 'tea-testing' department, who are responsible for all tea blending. This was a highly respected, and in a way, the prime department of the organisation. Changing a blend on the basis of the market requirements would create a 'blemish' on their knowledge as to what was the 'best' blend. To cut the whole story short, I was asked to fly down to Calcutta, and discuss the matter with the 'tea-testing' department. Fortunately for me, I already knew a couple of the tea-testers personally, since during my initial training programme I had spent three months in that department and fortunately I had kept up with them, even after moving to Sales, and out of Calcutta.

My line of argument which won the day was: If we can increase sales of *Yellow Label*, even with an inferior blend (according to them), the company would benefit in two ways. Firstly, through increased sales, and secondly, the blend would cost less (since it was made of inferior tea leaves). At long last the tea-testing department, agreed to give us a limited quantity of re-blended *Yellow Label* only for 'test marketing' in a limited number of tea shops within a restricted area. I accepted their proposition, and returned to Delhi.

Results of the Experiment

As they say, the rest is history. Within a couple of months after the experiment started, our sales of *Yellow Label* in those tea shops, went up. We started getting 50:50 business with Brooke Bond's *Red Label*. This was followed by a visit both from the 'Tea-Testing' Department, and the Marketing Controller from HO. After they satisfied themselves with the test marketing results, they went back to Calcutta to take a final decision regarding the change of blend in *Yellow Label* in the future. Initially, the change took place for all stocks going to the North region. Sales were monitored both at Branch and HO every month. *Yellow Label* showed progress quite dramatically. Of course, care was taken to brief the field force, who in turn briefed both the shopkeepers (dealers) and the tea shop owners. After about a year all further *Yellow Label* production switched over to the revised blend.

Moral of the Story

"The customer is always right" — he is the King. Give him what he wants, and you have a successful business.

Defining Target Customers' Income Classification – How Sacrosanct?

You ask a marketing man to define target customers for his product or brand, and he will give you demographic and psychographic details, which naturally include income classification. The latter is mainly required for pitching the marketing communication at the right target group. But for mature brands like *Horlicks* or *Nescafé*, how do you make sure that the communication or message will reach all such target customers, because in some cases, the brand awareness and loyalty have probably gone much beyond the stated target customers.

Let me give an example. Many years ago, when I was with HMM, I visited, as part of market work, a small town in Tamilnadu. As I was talking to a dealer (through our salesman), I noticed that the shopkeeper was handing over a bottle of *Horlicks* to an elderly lady. From her attire, which was just an ordinary saree, and nothing more, I realised that she was really poor. But how come she was paying for a bottle of *Horlicks*. How could she afford it if she was that poor? I became very curious, and requested our salesman to find out:

(1) for whom was she buying the *Horlicks* bottle, and,
(2) what did her husband or son do for a living?

I was told that the family were road construction workers, and that she was buying *Horlicks* for her grandson.

Naturally, I became even more interested in knowing what kind of income her family earned which enabled her to spend that kind of money on *Horlicks*. She confirmed that although they earned just enough to have two meals a day, since her grandchild was convalescing she felt that the child should have *Horlicks*, even if she had to forgo a meal.

Now, how do you plan the brand's communication strategy so as to include such customers? I have to admit that *Horlicks* is in fact a household name in Tamilnadu, so much so that if you visit a Tamilian's home he or she is likely to ask you whether you would like to have a cup of tea, coffee or *Horlicks*. Or, should we completely ignore any such incidents? I felt that the incident at least emphasised the need for marketing men to regularly visit markets. I am a great believer that the market teaches you a lot, particularly in a country like India, where the market dynamics are always fluctuating. Even if you cannot fully take care of incidents such as the one I have recounted, atleast you become aware of it. You might even find ways and means to cover such future customers in some other way.

On the basis of the above and similar experiences, we made it a policy to participate in village and small town fairs. Obviously 'word of mouth' is the best form of advertising, and participation in such fairs is one way to look for target customers who fall beyond the general income classification groups.

12

THE INDIAN EXPERIENCE

All case studies discussed in this book relate to the Indian Experience. Some of the Brands may have a foreign origin, such as *Horlicks, Maggi* or *Dettol*, but the discussion here has essentially to do with what has happened in the Indian sub-continent. Others, of course, are Indian brands. Among these, some are fast becoming global brands, like *Arvind Original Denim, Titan,* etc.

Not all case studies have been dealt with in the same way — this is intentional. In some cases, such as *Bacardi*, the conceptualisation is given in great detail. In some others, like *Boost*, the whole process as to how a new brand was launched have been dealt with in great detail in all its aspects.

Intentionally two cases of failure have also been included. Sometimes you learn more from failure than from a success story, provided you are able to analyse the reasons for such a failure. Also one must remember that all new product introductions are not a success. Far from it. In fact if you take a head count, there are probably more stories of failure than success.

It is important to remember that since the time, effort and cost that an organisation needs to spend, to develop a brand is enormous, it must be seen on a long- in fact, a very long-term perspective.

At the beginning of this book, while discussing 'branding', I had compared it with building a house. Maybe I can explain it further in terms of long-term investment and benefits. The house in which I live was built by the original owner in 1968. The brand *Horlicks*, which I sold from 1972 onwards was established in the '30s (in India through imports). The meticulous way in which the house was built has enabled me to continue living in it happily ever since I bought it in 1988. Similarly, because of the time and effort, and of course money, spent in a very systematic way to build the brand *Horlicks*, it is still not only a very big brand, (probably one of the biggest brands today in India), but it still continues to grow at the very ripe age of 100, thus giving enormous returns to the shareholders of the company.

But, of course, just as my house needs repairs and repainting from time to time, so too does the brand — sometimes a new creative approach, sometimes value addition to make the brand more valuable (to the consumer) or more contemporary. The operative word is "keeping in tune" with the changing aspirations of the brand's customers, so as to ensure their continuous Loyalty. Remember, it is loyalty which gives continuous business to the brand — the hallmark of 'success' for a brand. Therefore, one must remember that once established, the brand can give enormous payback, not only through the brand itself, but also through brand extensions. This particular aspect of the power of Brand Equity has been well-illustrated through the *Maggi, Dettol, Horlicks,* etc., case studies.

We all know that Advertising and Promotion play a very important role in building a brand. Of course, the importance of Market Research in this context cannot be over stressed. However, Distribution, particularly in a country like India plays a major role in brand-building. If the brand is not available at the usual place (dealer or shop), the shopkeeper will make sure to give an alternate product to his customer, thus breaking the chain that ensures customer loyalty. Remember, loyalty is a 'must' in the process of building a brand. Also remember, for certain kinds of products, the universe could extend across 5-7 lacs of outlets, and these require regular servicing.